The MUSHROOM COOKBOOK

The MUSHROOM COOKBOOK

Victoria Lloyd-Davies

TED SMART

A SALAMANDER BOOK

Published by Salamander Books Ltd,
129-137 York Way,
London N7 9LG,
United Kingdom

ISBN 1 85613 930 1

Specially produced for Ted Smart,
Guardian House, Borough Road,
Godalming, Surrey GU7 2AE.

CREDITS
Editor: Will Steeds
Designer: Louise Bruce
Photographer: Simon Butcher
Home economist: Wendy Dines
Stylist: Marian Price
Copy editor: Alison Leach
Index: Alison Leach
Typesetting: SX Composing Ltd., England
Colour Separation: P&W Graphics Pte. Ltd., Singapore
Printed in Belgium

Author: Victoria Lloyd-Davies
A Fellow of the Institute of Home Economics, Victoria is an experienced food writer and public relations consultant who is a regular contributor to magazines, newspapers and journals. She has concentrated on the promotion of food and is particularly interested in recipe development and food photography. For the last ten years she has specialized in the promotion of fresh cultivated mushrooms for the Mushroom Growers' Association. Victoria lives in central London and is married with two daughters.

When making any of the recipes in this book, you should follow either the metric or the Imperial measures as these are not interchangeable.
As seasoning is a matter of personal taste, salt and pepper have not been listed in the ingredients.

Contents

Foreword

by Antonio Carluccio

There are two good reasons for me to write the foreword to this book. First, because it deals with mushrooms and, although I am fanatical about wild mushrooms, I also appreciate and love the cultivated varieties. Second, but no less important, because I know that Victoria Lloyd-Davies has dedicated a great part of her life to the good cause of the mushroom.

Victoria is very interested in the mycological field, and with this book she demonstrates that besides commercial professionalism there is also an emotional part of herself ready to share a passion for loving and cooking this natural little wonder. I call mushrooms this because they still, whether cultivated or not, represent a sort of magic in the complexity of the botanical world.

Many mysteries are still to be discovered in the infinite mushroom world. For example, it is indeed intriguing to think about how a mushroom is constructed, how it reproduces and how it does so, so quickly. For mushrooms aren't able to use the sun's rays to nourish themselves like so many other plants – photosynthesis doesn't take place, as mushrooms contain no chlorophyll. All the energy and food for growing is taken from other matter.

The mystery lies in how mushrooms are transformed into something so very enjoyable and precious – like wine and bread, for example – from such matter. For it must be said that on top of taste and versatility in cooking they also represent one of the best forms of nourishment, low in fat and calories, high in proteins and minerals.

I jokingly used to say that cultivated mushrooms were bland compared to the wild variety. But in a world from which dozens of wild mushrooms disappear annually from the natural scene, it is most important not to joke any more about cultivated mushrooms but to appreciate the incredible work and research done by thousands of people all over the world to improve their quality still further. Their dedication means that we get more varieties, and of better quality, which we will be able to enjoy for a long time to come.

There are many books about cooking with wild mushrooms, but few about creating meals using cultivated ones. The Mushroom Cookbook, full of precious advice and suggestions for the better understanding of the culinary values of cultivated mushrooms, fills this gap admirably. The recipes are all fabulous and easy to prepare. It is intriguing how Victoria can turn an innocent button into a sort of devil, or arrange perfect marriages with fish, meat and cheese.

An important aspect of this book is how it refers to the preparation of mushrooms in a healthy way as either a starter or a main course for everybody, vegetarian or not.

Author's Introduction

There is no doubt that wild mushrooms picked in the fields in the early morning and cooked for breakfast are a great treat. Yet finding the right mushrooms is a specialist's task with dire consequences for those who make the wrong choice. It is all too easy for the inexperienced to make mistakes and pick the wrong mushrooms. The white cap mushrooms (Agaricus bisporus), generally seen in the shops today, are a very close relation to the field mushroom (Agaricus capestris), the wood mushroom (Agaricus silviola) and the horse mushroom (Agaricus arvensis). Cultivated mushrooms are 100% safe to eat and unlike their wild relations, which grow mainly in the spring and autumn and are killed off by frost, are available fresh every day of the year.

Mushroom growers, whether they have just small farms or are responsible for production on a massive scale, aim to replicate the same natural conditions that make mushrooms grow in the wild. They know that the consumer demands quality and different varieties of fresh mushrooms.

Cultivated mushrooms were first grown in England in the early 1880s. Most British mushroom growers now belong to the Mushroom Growers' Association which was set up in 1945 to promote the industry and develop better and more economic methods of growing cultivated mushrooms.

This book is a collection of almost a hundred recipes which I have created with the Mushroom Growers' Association. They range from the simplest of snacks – mushrooms on toast – to dishes which will delight your dinner guests; from quick and nutritious starters and salads to equally fast stir-fries; from comforting soups for a cold winter evening to kebabs cooked on a barbecue on a hot summer day. You will find traditional steak and mushroom pie or a modern mushroom and tomato tart made with filo pastry. There are also recipes for vegetarians and vegans which will be just as popular with non-vegetarians.

There is still a mystique about mushrooms, so I have included information about the buying, storing and preparation of mushrooms, explaining the differences in size and maturity of the white mushroom and introducing you to the cultivated speciality mushrooms now sold in some shops and supermarkets. I have recommended a particular type of mushroom for each recipe but this is primarily a matter of personal choice. If, for instance, you prefer the tightly closed white mushrooms, then use them in the recipes.

All the recipes use ingredients which are readily available and most are quick and easy to prepare. Cultivated mushrooms can be used to make hundreds of different dishes. Put them on your weekly shopping list and enjoy making the recipes in this book.

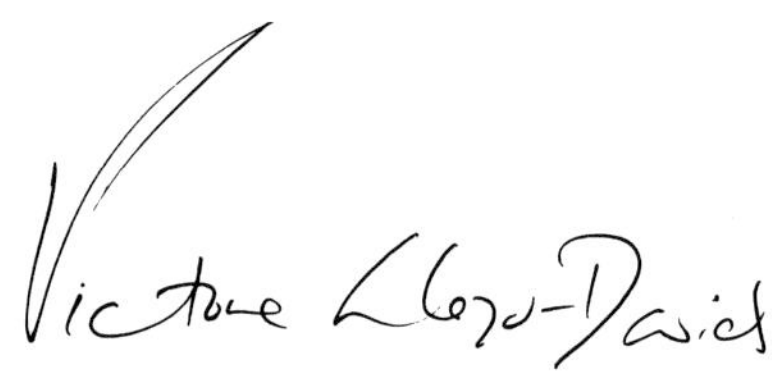

AGARICUS BISPORUS
White cap mushrooms are graded according to their size.

Button mushrooms are small and round with a tightly closed veil. They are pale in colour and firm to the touch. They range in size from 15 mm (5/8 inch) to 32 mm (1¼ inches).

Closed cup mushrooms are larger but are still round with a closed veil. They range in size from 32 mm (1¼ inches) to 60 mm (2⅜ inches) or more.

A wide variety of cultivated mushrooms is available today (left). Each has a unique flavour and texture, from the 'nutty' chestnut to the delicate-tasting small button.

Introduction

THE CULTIVATED MUSHROOM

Cultivated mushrooms are one of the most valuable horticultural crops grown in Great Britain. Over 98% of the fresh mushrooms sold in our shops are the white mushroom known as *Agaricus bisporus*. These are classified in four grades or sizes: button mushrooms, closed cup mushrooms, open cup mushrooms and large open mushrooms. The remaining 2% are comprised of speciality mushrooms. Chestnut mushrooms are similar to the white mushroom but they are brown and have a firmer texture and nutty flavour. They are available either as closed cup or flat mushrooms. Oyster mushrooms, which are fan-shaped, are generally brown but some are slate-grey, yellow or pink. Shiitake mushrooms are umbrella-like with dark brown caps and delicate white gills showing underneath.

GROWING CULTIVATED MUSHROOMS

Mushrooms are not a new vegetable. People have been eating them for centuries. The Pharaohs thought they were food from heaven; the Romans enjoyed them and they were considered an autumn feast from the Middle Ages to the Renaissance.

The first written accounts of how to grow cultivated mushrooms date from around 1650. Mushroom cultivation originated in France where they were grown in caves. Today, cultivated mushrooms are grown all year round in environmentally controlled growing houses on farms throughout the world.

The mushroom is the fruit body of a fungus. It grows from long, fine, white-grey threads (mycelium) in specially prepared compost. The manure comes from local stables or farms and is pasteurized to become a sweet-smelling, inert and natural medium for the growing fruit bodies. As both the temperature and humidity can now be controlled by the growers, we are able to eat mushrooms throughout the year. Mushrooms are grown naturally. Each crop takes about six weeks to mature, ready for picking – always by hand.

Most mushroom farms grow the white cap *Agaricus bisporus*. Many people are under the misapprehension that the four sizes of *Agaricus bisporus* are four different varieties. This is not so.

The mushroom doubles in size every 24 hours, so over a period of a week, a tiny button mushroom will develop into a closed cup mushroom, then to a larger open cup mushroom with its gills visible, and finally will become a large open or flat mushroom. As the size increases, the full mature flavour develops.

The chestnut or brown cap mushroom is grown like the white cap but the strain is slightly different, producing a mushroom with a brown outer skin.

Oyster mushrooms are cultivated on straw which is enclosed in black plastic bags. The grower makes holes in the bags and the mushrooms are thus encouraged to grow in clusters outside the bags, emulating their natural habitat of the trunks of trees.

Shiitake mushrooms were first grown in China and Japan. They used to be cultivated on dead or dying deciduous tree logs in Japan but today in Britain, they are grown on blocks of sawdust contained in a polythene mesh.

The grower decides when to pick the mushrooms according to the demands of the supermarkets or wholesale markets in meeting the needs of the consumer or caterer. Mushrooms are in the shops the day after they have been picked.

CHOOSING THE RIGHT MUSHROOM

First choose the right grade or size of mushroom for your recipe.

The small white button mushrooms have a delicate flavour and firm texture. They can be eaten raw in salads, served as a crudité for dips, used as a decorative garnish and are ideal for pale-coloured sauces.

The closed cup mushrooms are still firm and white but double the size of button mushrooms. They can be eaten raw or cooked. They are the most popular mushroom and are sold loose in the supermarkets. They can be marinated lightly for salads, threaded on to kebab skewers for barbecues, cooked whole with fish and chicken or sliced for pizzas or flans.

The open cup mushrooms are more mature in flavour and the gills can be seen under the caps. Open cups are very versatile, and are ideal for making garlic mushrooms or grilling as a vegetable, making soups and casseroles, or teaming with red meats and game.

Open cup mushrooms have a partly broken veil and pinkish gills visible under the cap. The mushrooms still retain their cup shape. They range in size from 40 mm (1⅝ inches) to 60 mm (2⅜ inches) or more.

Large open or flat mushrooms have completely broken veils, darker brown gills and flatter caps. The mushrooms are 'T'-shaped. They range in size from 40 mm (1⅝ inches) to 60 mm (2⅜ inches) or more.

AGARICUS BISPORUS
(syn. *A. BRUNNESCENS*)
Chestnut or brown cap mushrooms.

Closed cup chestnut mushrooms are round with closed veils. They range in size from 25 mm (1 inch) to 65 mm (2⅝ inches) and when sold are graded as small, standard and large chestnut mushrooms.

Flat chestnut mushrooms range in size from under 75 mm (3 inches) to 150 mm (6 inches). They are available as small, under 75 mm (3 inches), the most popular size, as medium, from 75 mm (3 inches) to 100 mm (4 inches), and as large, over 100 mm (4 inches).

The large open mushrooms are fully mature with a rich flavour. They can range from 7.5 cm/3 inches in diameter up to the size of a meat plate. They are perfect for stuffing with different mixtures, or for slicing and cooking with traditional bacon and eggs or steak. Their flavour also makes them ideal to use in stuffings for a Sunday roast.

The closed cup and **flat chestnut mushrooms** can be used instead of the **white mushrooms.** They need the same preparation but they have a firmer texture and stronger, more nutty flavour. They hold their shape well when cooked and do not release as much moisture.

Oyster mushrooms have a delicate flavour and texture. They can be eaten raw but are usually cooked. They can be used whole or sliced and can replace white mushrooms in most recipes, particularly stir-fries, fish dishes and in creamy sauces. They are good fried, grilled or baked.

Shiitake mushrooms have dark brown umbrella-shaped caps with pure white gills. They have a unique steak-like texture and a subtle meaty flavour. They can be eaten raw, in which case you will detect a faint peppery bite, but they are generally cooked. Their slightly slippery texture particularly enhances Chinese and oriental dishes. Their strong flavour makes them the ideal choice for special dark mushroom sauces; shiitake and Madeira are perfect partners.

More varieties of cultivated speciality mushrooms are coming into the shops. Keep a look out for **Enoki, Jew's Ear, Blue Leg** and **Blewitts.**

BUYING AND STORING MUSHROOMS

Fresh mushrooms need careful handling. If treated roughly, they can bruise and valuable nutrients will be lost. Mushrooms are harvested by hand; they are trimmed, graded and packed into different sizes of container. The containers are checked for weight before being covered with lids showing details of the contents, grower's brand name and address. These mushrooms are sold loose in shops and markets. Many of the mushrooms sold direct to supermarkets are packed in punnets at the mushroom farm with labels giving the relevant weight.

Take care when selecting mushrooms in a shop. Handle them as little as possible and avoid putting any heavy items on top of them in your shopping basket or supermarket trolley.

Mushrooms should be stored in the salad drawer of a refrigerator. They should never be washed before storing – just remove the cling film from the punnet and cover the mushrooms with absorbent kitchen paper. If you buy them loose in plastic bags, transfer them gently into a paper bag. See page 15 for information on freezing mushrooms.

All mushrooms are best when eaten fresh but they will keep for a few days in a refrigerator. The different grades of white mushrooms should be eaten within five days of purchase. Chestnut mushrooms last slightly longer, about a week. Oyster mushrooms will keep for three or four days and shiitake mushrooms should be eaten within six days.

PREPARATION

Mushrooms are normally perfectly clean; any dark specks on them are peat. It is best to rinse them quickly in a colander, under cold running water, just before you eat or cook them.

Never peel cultivated mushrooms or remove their stalks. The whole mushroom is edible and the skin contains nutrients and flavour. The mushroom is a single structure so it is damaged if the stalk is pulled out. If you like stuffed mushrooms, trim the stalk back slightly, then mould the stuffing around the stalk using it as a firm support.

Cultivated mushrooms can be eaten raw or cooked. They can be eaten whole, sliced thickly, halved or quartered. Always slice mushrooms downwards through the cap to the stalk, using a sharp pointed knife. A sprinkling of lemon juice will help to retain the delicate pale colour of button or closed cup mushrooms.

NUTRITION

Mushrooms are an important part of a healthy diet. The full nutritional value is obtained when eaten raw or lightly cooked.

- **Low in calories**
  Less than 30 calories (110 kj) per 100 g (4 oz). Useful in slimming diets as mushrooms also provide some fibre which promotes the 'satiety' factor.

PLEUROTUS

Oyster mushrooms are fan-shaped and vary in size from 60 mm (2⅜ inches) to 100 mm (4 inches). They grow in clusters of overlapping tiers, like roof tiles. They vary in colour from dark brown to slate-grey and some are bright yellow. The gills are white and they have short solid stems.

Pleurotus ostreatus *– grey oyster mushrooms*

Pleurotus pulmonarius *– dark brown oyster mushrooms*

Pleurotus citrinopileatus – yellow oyster mushrooms

LENTINUS EDODES

Shiitake mushrooms have brown umbrella-shaped caps, with pure white gills underneath, and relatively thick stems. They range in size from 30mm (1⅛ inches) to 75 mm (3 inches).

- **Vegetable protein**
  Mushroom protein is distinctly superior to other vegetable proteins because of its essential amino acid content. *Agaricus bisporus,* the white mushroom, ranks above all other vegetables, except beans, peas and lentils, in its essential amino acid content. Between 70 and 90% of the vegetable protein present can be easily digested.

- **Good source of minerals**
  Particularly potassium which is a great asset to the elderly as their diet tends to be restricted.

- **Good source of vitamins**
  Vegans should note that mushrooms and yeast are their sole sources of vital B12.

- **Low in salt**
  Solves the 'taste' problem of a low-salt diet. Mushrooms add flavour to food cooked without salt.

- **Low in fat and no cholesterol**
  Excellent eating for a healthy heart!

AGARICUS BISPORUS		
	Average value per 100g/4oz	
	Energy	110kj (30 calories)
	Protein	3g
	Fat	0.2g
	Cholesterol	nil
	Sugar	trace
VITAMINS	B1 (Thiamine)	0.1mg
	B2 (Riboflavin)	0.4mg
	Niacin	0.5mg
	Pantothenic Acid	6.2mg
	Folic Acid	0.016mg
	B12	0.05mg
	Vitamin C	2mg
MINERALS	Phosphorus	75mg
	Potassium	620mg
	Iron	1mg
	Copper	1mg
	Zinc	0.86mg
	Selinium	Trace
	Salt	6mg
	Dietary Fibre	1g

COOKING WITH MUSHROOMS

- The average portion of raw mushrooms is 100 g (4 oz). As a cooked vegetable, allow 175 g (6 oz).
- Sliced button mushrooms are excellent for sandwich fillings.
- Dip button mushrooms into cheese fondue for a meal or into yogurt for a snack.
- Mushrooms are ideal for slimmers. They have only 30 calories per 100 g (4 oz) portion.
- The larger the mushrooms, the more mature the flavour. They complement meat and game.
- Trimmed mushroom stalks should be used to make stocks and consommés.
- Chestnut mushrooms have a higher percentage of dry matter. They are excellent when making mushroom pâtés, breads and pastries.
- Cook a few open cup mushrooms around the Sunday roast for the last 10 minutes of cooking.
- Mushrooms can be cooked on a hob, under a grill, in an oven, in a microwave, or on a barbecue.
- Mushrooms should always be cooked quickly, particularly when frying them – otherwise, they will absorb all the fat and lose their flavour.
- Mushrooms do not need long cooking. Add them to casseroles for the last 20 minutes.
- Quartered or roughly chopped mushrooms make a good alternative to minced beef for vegetarians.
- Choose closed cup mushrooms to 'turn' for special occasions. Make a series of curved cuts from the top of each mushroom cap to the base. Remove a narrow strip of peel along each cut.
- Sliced mushrooms make an attractive garnish for other dishes; soups, grilled fish or steaks.
- Speciality mushrooms have lovely shapes and colours – excellent for entertaining.
- Mushrooms make 'alternative' starters. Coat them with seafood mayonnaise and serve instead of prawn cocktail. Poach them in white wine, then toss in garlic butter and serve instead of snails.
- Closed cup mushrooms should always be marinated well before barbecueing.
- The flat chestnut mushrooms, stuffed and wrapped in foil, cook well on barbecues.
- Raw mushrooms taste delicious in salads but if you prefer the texture of cooked mushrooms, poach them for 5 minutes in wine or fruit juice, then chill them in the chosen liquid. Remove the mushrooms with a slotted spoon.
- Marinated mushrooms keep well for five days in an airtight container in the refrigerator, making them an ideal vegetable to prepare in advance for dinner parties or celebration buffets.
- Bargain hunters can buy bulk supplies from local farm shops. It is best to freeze mushrooms sliced rather than whole. Sauté sliced mushrooms quickly in a little butter or oil. Drain them on absorbent kitchen paper. Open freeze the mushrooms on trays, then transfer them into freezer bags. Store for up to three months. Use straight from the freezer for pies and casseroles.
- For every 450 g (1 lb) of mushrooms, allow 50 g (2 oz) of both shallots and butter to make duxelle. Cook the chopped mushrooms and shallots in the butter over a moderate heat, stirring occasionally, until all the liquid has evaporated and the mixture is dry. Season lightly. Pack into ice-cube trays and freeze until firm. Then transfer the cubes of duxelle into freezer bags. Store for up to three months. Use like stock cubes to flavour gravy, soups, sauces and stuffings.
- Mushrooms can also be pickled and preserved in oil. See recipe on page 78.

Soups and Starters

Mushroom soup can be light and creamy in colour or robust and comforting. You can make it in bulk, using less liquid, freezing it in concentrated form and adding the remaining liquid when it is reheated. Mushrooms make excellent hot and cold starters. They are particularly good marinated and chilled – ideal when entertaining as you can prepare them in advance.

Mushroom filo baskets

Grease four upturned 175 ml/6 fl oz ramekins (or metal moulds) lightly. Drape one half sheet of filo pastry over a ramekin, brush with melted butter and press the overhanging edges back on to the pastry on the ramekin. Cover with another half sheet of pastry and brush with melted butter. Repeat with the remaining pastry and ramekins. Place on a baking sheet and bake in a preheated 180°C (350°F/gas mark 4) oven for 15 minutes.

To make the filling, heat the oil and cook the spring onions, carrots, pepper, mushrooms and root ginger for 5 minutes, stirring. Stir in the asparagus, bean sprouts and soy sauce. Cook for a further 3 minutes, then pile into the pastry cases. **Serves 4**

Mushroom hors d'oeuvre

Put the mushrooms into a mixing bowl with 30 ml (2 tbsp) of the lemon juice, the spring onions, sunflower seeds and seasoning. Mix well and chill. Just before serving, remove the stone and peel from the avocado, then slice the flesh and sprinkle with the remaining lemon juice. Arrange the avocado slices on individual serving plates with the mushroom salad. **Serves 4-6**

Right: Mushroom filo baskets.

INGREDIENTS

50 g (2 oz) unsalted butter, melted
4 sheets filo pastry, cut in half widthways

FILLING

30 ml (2 tbsp) oil
50 g (2 oz) spring onions, finely chopped
75 g (3 oz) young carrots, sliced
½ orange pepper, seeded and cut into small strips
225 g (8 oz) button mushrooms
5-7.5 ml (1-1½ tsp) grated fresh root ginger
50 g (2 oz) asparagus sprue, chopped
50 g (2 oz) fresh bean sprouts
30 ml (2 tbsp) light soy sauce

225 g (8 oz) button mushrooms, sliced
45 ml (3 tbsp) lemon juice
4 spring onions, chopped
15 ml (1 tbsp) sunflower seeds, toasted
1 ripe avocado

Rich mushroom soup

Melt the butter in a large saucepan, add the mushrooms and cook for 3 minutes. Add the flour and stir well to coat the mushrooms. Stir in the stock and milk and bring to the boil slowly. Cover the pan and simmer for 5 minutes. Leave to cool, then purée in a blender. Season to taste.

Chill if serving cold or reheat if serving hot. Pour into soup bowls and stir in the cream. Garnish with parsley. **Serves 6**

Crispy chicken with mustard sauce

Combine the chicken, mushrooms, parsley and seasoning together. Shape into 16 7.5 cm (3 inch) sausages. Chill. Mix the breadcrumbs and sesame seeds together. Dip each sausage into the beaten egg, then coat with the breadcrumb mixture. Chill.

Just before serving, mix the sauce ingredients together. Deep fry the sausages for about 5 minutes, or until golden brown and cooked through to the centre. Serve with the sauce. **Serves 4**

Mushroom and seafood special

Arrange the mushrooms, cap side down, in a lightly oiled roasting tin. Cut the haddock into small pieces and mix with the prawns, breadcrumbs, oyster sauce and egg yolk. Divide between the mushrooms and sprinkle with cheese. Bake in a preheated 200°C (400°F/gas mark 6) oven.for 10 minutes. **Serves 4**

Top left: Crispy chicken with mustard sauce; Rich mushroom soup (top right); Mushroom and seafood special (bottom).

INGREDIENTS

50 g (2 oz) butter
450 g (1 lb) closed cup mushrooms, thickly sliced
40 g (1½ oz) plain flour
300 ml (½ pint) vegetable stock
600 ml (1 pint) milk
150 ml (¼ pint) single cream

225 g (8 oz) fresh chicken breast, minced
225 g (8 oz) large open mushrooms, very finely chopped
30 ml (2 tbsp) chopped fresh parsley
50 g (2 oz) fresh white breadcrumbs
60 ml (4 tbsp) sesame seeds
1 egg (size 2), beaten
oil for frying

SAUCE

250 g (9 oz) low-fat fromage frais
20 ml (4 tsp) horseradish mustard
15 ml (1 tbsp) lemon juice

8 large open cup mushrooms
5 ml (1 tsp) oil
225 g (8 oz) haddock fillet
125 g (4 oz) peeled cooked prawns
50 g (2 oz) fresh white breadcrumbs
5 ml (1 tsp) oyster sauce
1 egg yolk, beaten
75 g (3 oz) Cheddar cheese, grated

Ginger, split pea and mushroom soup

Put the onion, ginger, coriander, split peas and stock into a saucepan. Bring to the boil, cover and simmer gently for 30 minutes. Add the mushrooms and simmer for a further 15 minutes. Season to taste and serve garnished with lemon slices and sprigs of coriander. **Serves 4-6**

INGREDIENTS

1 onion, finely chopped
15 ml (1 tbsp) grated fresh root ginger
30 ml (2 tbsp) chopped fresh coriander
225 (8 oz) green split peas
1.1 litres (2 pints) vegetable stock
275 g (10 oz) button mushrooms, sliced

Country soup

Heat the oil and cook the onion for 1 minute. Add the mushrooms and cook for a further minute. Stir in the stock, lemon rind and parsley. Bring to the boil and simmer for 5 minutes. Stir in the breadcrumbs and seasoning and cook for 1 minute. Remove from the heat and stir in the soured cream. Reheat gently but do not allow to boil. **Serves 6**

30 ml (2 tbsp) oil
1 onion, chopped
225 g (8 oz) large open mushrooms, finely chopped
1.1 litres (2 pints) vegetable stock
grated rind of 1 lemon
45 ml (3 tbsp) chopped parsley
125 g (4 oz) fresh wholemeal breadcrumbs
30 ml (2 tbsp) soured cream

Mushroom chowder

Melt the butter in a large saucepan. Add the onions, celery, garlic, potatoes and carrots and cook for 5 minutes, stirring occasionally. Add the stock, milk, mushrooms and haddock and bring to the boil slowly. Add the peas and sweetcorn and bring back to the boil slowly. Cover the pan and simmer for 5 minutes. Season to taste. **Serves 8**

25 g (1 oz) butter
2 onions, finely chopped
4 sticks celery, finely chopped
1 clove garlic, finely chopped
450 g (1 lb) potatoes, diced
175 g (6 oz) carrots, diced
600 ml (1 pint) hot vegetable stock
300 ml (½ pint) milk
450 g (1 lb) closed cup mushrooms, quartered
225 g (8 oz) haddock fillet, cut into small pieces
125 g (4 oz) fresh or frozen peas
225 g (8 oz) can sweetcorn, drained

Right: Mushroom chowder.

Coriander mushrooms

Squeeze half the lemon juice over the mushrooms. Crush the coriander seeds with a rolling pin. Heat 45 ml (3 tbsp) of the olive oil in a frying pan and add the crushed coriander seeds. Cook gently for a few seconds, then add the mushrooms, bay leaves and seasoning. Stir-fry for 1 minute. Cover the pan and cook over a low heat for 5 minutes. Transfer to a serving dish and pour the remaining olive oil and lemon juice over the mushrooms. Serve hot or cold with crusty bread. **Serves 4**

INGREDIENTS

juice of ½ lemon
450 g (1 lb) chestnut mushrooms, quartered
15 ml (1 tbsp) coriander seeds
60 ml (4 tbsp) olive oil
4 bay leaves

Baked mushroom puddings with tomato sauce

Heat the oil and fry the mushrooms and onion for 5 minutes, stirring occasionally. Put into a food processor and blend until smooth. Add the remaining ingredients and blend for 15 seconds. Turn into four large greased ramekins. Cover with foil, then bake in a preheated 180°C (350°F/gas mark 4) oven for about 25 minutes until quite firm.

To make the sauce, put the ingredients into a saucepan. Bring to the boil, cover the pan and simmer for 15 minutes. Remove the lid, then boil rapidly for about 8 minutes until the mixture is fairly thick. Press through a sieve or blend in a food processor until smooth. Return to the pan and keep warm. Spoon the sauce on to 4 serving plates, then invert the mushroom puddings on top. Garnish with watercress. **Serves 4**

30 ml (2 tbsp) oil
350 g (12 oz) open cup mushrooms, chopped
1 onion, chopped
1 egg (size 3), beaten
45 ml (3 tbsp) milk
10 ml (2 tsp) Dijon mustard

SAUCE

225 g (8 oz) carrots, chopped
400 g (14 oz) can peeled chopped tomatoes
1 onion, chopped

GARNISH

small sprigs of watercress

Top right: Coriander mushrooms; Baked mushroom puddings with tomato sauce (bottom).

Mushroom fruit salad

INGREDIENTS

2 oranges
225 g (8 oz) button mushrooms
25 g (1 oz) flaked almonds
175 g (6 oz) strawberries, sliced
½ lemon
½ cucumber, sliced
15 ml (1 tbsp) finely chopped mint
GARNISH
sprig of mint

Peel 1 orange and remove the pith. Cut the orange into rings, then into quarters. Mix with the mushrooms, flaked almonds and strawberries. Squeeze the juice from the remaining orange and the ½ lemon and pour over the mushrooms. Arrange the cucumber around the edge of the salad bowl and put the mushroom mixture in the centre. Sprinkle with chopped mint and garnish with the sprig of mint. Chill for 1 hour. **Serves 4**

Mushroom pâté

150 g (5 oz) butter
1 onion, finely chopped
2 cloves garlic
450 g (1 lb) chestnut mushrooms, finely chopped
TO SERVE
triangles of toast

Melt 25 g (1 oz) of the butter in a pan and fry the onion and garlic gently until almost cooked, then add the mushrooms and continue frying until the onions and mushrooms are cooked. Increase the heat and cook very quickly to evaporate any liquid, stirring frequently. Season well with salt and pepper and turn into individual dishes. Chill. Melt the remaining butter and pour over pâté. Chill before serving with toast. **Serves 4**

Marinated mushrooms

125 ml (4 fl oz) wine vinegar
½ clove garlic
1 bay leaf
1 small onion, finely chopped
30 ml (2 tbsp) tomato purée
45 ml (3 tbsp) oil
450 g (1 lb) button mushrooms
GARNISH
fresh coriander

Put the vinegar, garlic, bay leaf and onion into a saucepan. Bring to the boil and simmer until the onion is tender. Add the tomato purée and oil. Mix together thoroughly and season to taste. Pour the marinade over the mushrooms, cover and leave overnight in the refrigerator. Remove the garlic and bay leaf. Serve in individual dishes, garnished with coriander. **Serves 4**

Right: Marinated mushrooms.

Salads

You do not have to cook mushrooms. The small crunchy button mushrooms taste delicious in salads. Rinse them in a colander under cold running water just before you eat them. If you prefer mushrooms to be slightly softer, marinate them in French dressing for a couple of hours, or poach them lightly in a little wine and chill them, then toss them into salads.

Mushroom and alfalfa salad with garlic croûtons

INGREDIENTS

4 slices white bread, buttered on both sides and crusts removed
a little garlic powder
450 g (1 lb) button mushrooms, halved
125 g (4 oz) alfalfa sprouts
150 g (5 oz) radishes, quartered
225 g (8 oz) mooli, grated
celery leaves
1 fennel bulb, chopped

Sprinkle the buttered bread lightly with garlic powder and toast under a preheated grill. Cut into small cubes. Toss all the prepared vegetables together and scatter the garlic croûtons over the top. **Serves 6**

Eggs with radicchio and mushrooms

2 small radicchio
1 head fennel, cut in half and finely sliced
125 g (4 oz) open cup mushrooms, thickly sliced
6 hard-boiled eggs, quartered
15 ml (1 tbsp) chopped parsley
30 ml (2 tbsp) lemon juice
15 ml (1 tbsp) Worcestershire sauce

Tear the radicchio leaves into a salad bowl. Add the fennel, mushrooms, eggs and parsley. Whisk the remaining ingredients together and pour over the salad, then toss well. **Serves 4**

Top right: Eggs with radicchio and mushrooms; Mushroom and alfalfa salad with garlic croûtons (bottom).

Cracked wheat salad

Put the cracked wheat, wine and water into a saucepan. Cover and bring to the boil, then simmer, uncovered, for 20 minutes or until the liquid has been absorbed.

Meanwhile, slice the mushrooms thickly and toss in vinaigrette dressing. Core and slice the apples and toss lightly in lemon juice. Cut the cheese into small cubes. Arrange the salad on individual plates and serve. **Serves 4**

Mushroom and fennel salad

Cook the mange tout in boiling water until just tender, then drain and toss in the French dressing while still warm. Cool.

Arrange the pepper rings on four plates. Fill each pepper ring with the mushrooms and fennel. Arrange the mange tout on the plates. Blend the mayonnaise with the soured cream, herbs and seasoning. Place a portion of herb mayonnaise in the centre of each plate. **Serves 4**

Italian salad

Put the wine, water, bay leaves, black peppercorns and lemon rind into a saucepan and bring to the boil. Set aside for 10 minutes, then strain into a mixing bowl. Add the mushrooms, then chill for at least 1 hour, stirring occasionally.

Cook the beans in boiling water for 3 minutes. Rinse under cold water and drain well. Arrange the salami, beans and endive on individual plates with the mushrooms in the centre. **Serves 4**

Right: Mushroom and fennel salad.

INGREDIENTS

175 g (6 oz) cracked wheat
300 ml (½ pint) red wine
150 ml (¼ pint) water
450 g (1 lb) small closed cup mushrooms
vinaigrette dressing
2 apples, cored and sliced
lemon juice
175 g (6 oz) Sage Derby cheese

225 g (8 oz) mange tout, stringed
30 ml (2 tbsp) French dressing
1 each green, yellow and red pepper, seeded and cut into rings
225 g (8 oz) small closed cup mushrooms, sliced
50 g (2 oz) bulb fennel, diced
45 ml (3 tbsp) mayonnaise
45 ml (3 tbsp) soured cream
60 ml (4 tbsp) chopped parsley
30 ml (2 tbsp) chopped fresh tarragon
30 ml (2 tbsp) snipped fresh chives

90 ml (6 tbsp) white wine
30 ml (2 tbsp) water
3 bay leaves
5 ml (1 tsp) black peppercorns
strip of lemon rind
450 g (1 lb) button mushrooms
125 g (4 oz) dwarf stick beans
125 g (4 oz) salami, sliced
curly endive or crisp lettuce, shredded

Summer salad

Peel the garlic, slice and crush it with a pinch of salt on a board with a palette knife until it is smooth and creamy. Mix together the garlic, vinegar, oil and pepper and marinate the mushrooms in the sauce for several hours or overnight.

Halve the avocados and remove the stones and peel. Slice the avocados and toss in lemon juice. Arrange the avocado and curly endive on plates with the marinated mushrooms. **Serves 4**

Mushroom and celeriac salad

Put the egg yolk into a mixing bowl and whisk in the olive oil gradually until the mixture is pale and thick. Then whisk in the vinegar, soured cream and seasoning. Fold in the mushrooms, celeriac and carrot. Chill before serving, garnished with parsley. **Serves 4-6**

Tossed mushroom and walnut salad

Cook the haricots verts in boiling water for 2 minutes. Rinse with cold water, then drain well. Sprinkle the pears with a little lemon juice. Mix the walnuts, mushrooms, lettuce, haricots verts and pears in a salad bowl. Whisk together the ingredients for the dressing, pour over the salad and then toss. **Serves 4**

Top right: Summer salad; Tossed mushroom and walnut salad (centre left); Mushroom and celeriac salad (bottom).

INGREDIENTS

2 cloves garlic
60 ml (4 tbsp) red wine vinegar
90 ml (6 tbsp) sunflower oil
450 g (1 lb) chestnut mushrooms
2 avocados
lemon juice
curly endive

1 egg yolk
150 ml (¼ pint) olive oil
30 ml (2 tbsp) white wine vinegar
150 ml (¼ pint) soured cream
350 g (12 oz) button mushrooms, halved
½ large celeriac root, peeled and coarsely grated
225 g (8 oz) carrots, coarsely grated

125 g (4 oz) haricots verts, topped and tailed
2 ripe pears, peeled, cored and roughly chopped
lemon juice
125 g (4 oz) walnut halves
450 g (1 lb) button mushrooms
1 lollo rosso lettuce, washed, well drained and torn into small pieces

DRESSING

45 ml (3 tbsp) sesame oil
45 ml (3 tbsp) cider vinegar
10 ml (2 tsp) soft dark brown sugar

Warm mushroom and turkey liver salad

Arrange the endive on individual plates. Heat 15 ml (1 tbsp) of the oil and brown the pine kernels, then remove. Heat the remaining oil and cook the turkey livers over a medium heat for about 3 minutes. Add the mushrooms and cook for a further 3 minutes, stirring occasionally. Remove the turkey livers and slice quickly (the inside should still be pink). Add the vinegar and seasoning to the pan with the pine kernels and turkey livers. Heat through, then serve on top of the endive. **Serves 4-6**

Mushroom and seafood salad

Pour the wine over the mushrooms. Add the thyme and seasoning and mix well. Cover and chill for 2 hours. Mix the remaining ingredients together. Stir in the mushrooms with any juices, and toss together. **Serves 4**

Chicken salad

Put the oil, vinegar, marjoram and seasoning into a saucepan. Bring to the boil, then pour into a mixing bowl with the mushrooms. Mix well, then leave until cold, stirring occasionally.

Wash and drain the endive or lettuce, then tear into small pieces. Toss with the chicken, grapes and radishes. Arrange the salad around the edge of a serving platter, then pile the mushroom mixture in the centre. **Serves 4**

Top: Chicken salad; Warm mushroom and turkey liver salad (centre); Mushroom and seafood salad (bottom).

INGREDIENTS

½ small curly endive
30 ml (2 tbsp) oil
25 g (1 oz) pine kernels
225 g (8 oz) turkey livers
225 g (8 oz) chestnut mushrooms, quartered
30 ml (2 tbsp) red wine vinegar

75 ml (5 tbsp) white wine
350 g (12 oz) button mushrooms
10 ml (2 tsp) chopped fresh thyme
175 g (6 oz) bean sprouts, blanched in boiling water for 15 seconds, then drained
175 g (6 oz) peeled cooked prawns
125 g (4 oz) oceansticks, each cut into 3
175 g (6 oz) cucumber, sliced

30 ml (2 tbsp) olive oil
60 ml (4 tbsp) red wine vinegar
10 ml (2 tsp) chopped fresh marjoram
450 g (1 lb) button or small closed cup mushrooms
curly endive or crisp lettuce
225 g (8 oz) cooked chicken, diced
175 g (6 oz) grapes, halved and pips removed
8 large radishes, halved and sliced

Mushroom, ham and pasta salad

Cook the pasta according to the packet instructions. Drain and cool. Mix the pasta, cucumber, ham, mushrooms and tomatoes together. Whisk the remaining ingredients together, then pour the dressing on to the salad and mix well. Chill for 3-4 hours before serving so that the mushroom mixture is marinated in the dressing. Turn the salad carefully after 2 hours and again just before serving. **Serves 4**

INGREDIENTS

225 g (8 oz) pasta spirals
½ cucumber, cut into thin matchsticks
125 g (4 oz) piece ham, cubed
350 g (12 oz) button mushrooms
225 g (8 oz) tomatoes, peeled, seeded, then chopped
30 ml (2 tbsp) oil
15 ml (1 tbsp) vinegar
15 ml (1 tbsp) chopped fresh oregano

Spinach, mushroom and bacon salad

Pick over the spinach very carefully and remove all the stalks and any large tough or discoloured leaves. Wash thoroughly in cold water and drain well. Grill the bacon until it is really crisp. Leave to cool and then cut into small pieces.

Arrange the spinach in a large salad bowl. Halve the avocado and remove the stone and skin. Slice the avocado thinly and toss in lemon juice. Arrange the avocado slices on the spinach. Add the mushrooms and sprinkle with bacon and chives or spring onions. Mix all the dressing ingredients in a screw-top jar and shake well. Just before serving pour over the salad. **Serves 4**

225 g (8 oz) fresh small-leaf spinach
175 g (6 oz) streaky bacon
1 avocado
juice of ½ lemon
450 g (1 lb) small button mushrooms
15 ml (1 tbsp) snipped fresh chives or chopped spring onions

DRESSING

60 ml (4 tbsp) olive or salad oil
15 ml (1 tbsp) dry sherry
15 ml (1 tbsp) lemon juice
grated lemon rind
pinch of caster sugar
pinch of dry mustard
freshly ground black pepper

Top right: Mushroom, ham and pasta salad; Spinach, mushroom and bacon salad (bottom left).

Main Meals

Mushrooms make a meal. Serve them as a vegetable, grilled or poached, or add them to your favourite recipes. The paler, closed cup mushrooms are best with fish and chicken whilst the more mature open mushrooms complement red meats. Mushrooms are also marvellous in stir-fries. They hold their shape and enjoy being cooked quickly over a high heat.

Courgette and mushroom fettucini

Heat the oil and cook the courgettes, onion, garlic and mushrooms in a covered saucepan over a gentle heat for a few minutes. Stir in the tomatoes, herbs, turmeric and sherry. Bring to the boil and simmer gently for 5 minutes. Add the cream and seasoning, and simmer for a further 20 minutes.

Meanwhile, cook the fettucini according to the instructions on the packet. Serve the courgette and mushroom mixture on top of the fettucini. **Serves 4**

Sauté of pork in cider

Heat the oil in a wok, add the beans, cover and cook for about 3 minutes. Add the pork and onion and cook for a further 3 minutes. Stir in the mushrooms and cook for a minute. Stir in the cider, sage, olives and seasoning. Cook for about 5 minutes. Blend the cornflour with a little water, then stir into the pork mixture. Bring to the boil, then serve on a bed of rice. **Serves 4**

Right: Courgette and mushroom fettucini.

INGREDIENTS

30 ml (2 tbsp) oil
350 g (12 oz) courgettes, sliced
1 onion, sliced
2 cloves garlic, crushed
350 g (12 oz) closed cup mushrooms, sliced
225 g (8 oz) can peeled chopped tomatoes
2.5 ml (½ tsp) dried basil
2.5 ml (½ tsp) dried mint
5 ml (1 tsp) turmeric
75 ml (5 tbsp) sherry
150 ml (¼ pint) double cream
225 g (8 oz) fettucini

30 ml (2 tbsp) oil
175 g (6 oz) dwarf stick beans, cut into 5 cm (2 inch) lengths
450 g (1 lb) pork fillet, cut into narrow strips
1 large onion, cut into narrow wedge-shaped strips
350 g (12 oz) open cup mushrooms, sliced
60 ml (4 tbsp) strong medium-dry cider
15 ml (1 tbsp) chopped fresh sage
12 pimento-stuffed olives
5-10 ml (1-2 tsp) cornflour

Steak and mushroom pie

Cut the steak into 2.5 cm (1 inch) cubes and coat in the seasoned flour. Put half the steak into a 1.4 litre (2½ pint) pie dish. Add the onion, mushrooms and herbs, then fill the dish with the remaining meat but do not pack it tightly. Pour in enough stock to three-quarter fill the dish. Roll out the pastry and use to cover the pie dish. Brush with beaten egg. Bake in a preheated 220°C (425°F/gas mark 7) oven for 30 minutes; then reduce the oven temperature to 190°C (375°F/gas mark 5), cover the pie with a sheet of wet greaseproof paper and continue cooking for at least a further 1¼ hours until the meat is tender. Check by inserting a skewer through the pastry into the meat. **Serves 4**

Chicken and mushroom pie

To make the pastry, rub the margarine into the flour and salt until the mixture resembles fine breadcrumbs. Add enough cold water to make a stiff dough. Cover and chill.

To make the filling, cut the skinned and boned chicken portions into large pieces and coat in the flour. Put into a 1.1 litre (2 pint) pie dish with the mushrooms, carrots and red pepper. Mix together the chicken stock, grated lemon rind, lemon juice and black pepper. Pour over the chicken.

Roll out the pastry and use to cover the pie dish. Make two slits in the centre of the pastry. Use the pastry trimmings to make leaves and arrange on top of the pastry. Brush the pastry with a little milk and bake in a preheated 220°C (425°F/gas mark 7) oven for 15 minutes; then reduce the oven temperature to 190°C (375°F/gas mark 5) and cook for a further 40 minutes. **Serves 6**

Top left: Steak and mushroom pie; Chicken and mushroom pie (bottom right).

INGREDIENTS

575 g (1¼ lb) stewing steak
25 g (1 oz) seasoned flour
1 onion, sliced
450 g (1 lb) large open mushrooms
2.5 ml (½ tsp) mixed dried herbs
about 350 ml (12 fl oz) beef stock
275 g (10 oz) flaky pastry
beaten egg, to glaze

PASTRY

125 g (4 oz) margarine
225 g (8 oz) plain flour
pinch of salt
about 45 ml (3 tbsp) cold water

FILLING

6 chicken portions, skinned and boned
50 g (2 oz) plain flour
450 g (1 lb) closed cup mushrooms, sliced
4 carrots, sliced
1 red pepper, seeded and chopped
300 ml (½ pint) chicken stock
grated rind of 1 lemon
15 ml (1 tbsp) lemon juice
black pepper
milk, to glaze

Honey-glazed pork and mushrooms

This recipe is ideal for people with limited cooking facilities – for example, in holiday accommodation or on a boat. Cook the chops in a non-stick frying pan over a gentle heat for about 2 minutes on each side. Stir in the honey, mustard and mushrooms. Cover the pan and cook gently for 8-10 minutes, turning the chops over halfway through the cooking time. Serve sprinkled with parsley. **Serves 2**

Lamb with mushroom and orange sauce

Mix the ingredients for the marinade together, then pour over the chops. Cover and chill for at least 4 hours, turning the chops over occasionally. Remove the chops from the marinade, reserving the juices.

To make the sauce, heat the oil and cook the onion and garlic until soft. Stir in the mushrooms and cook for a further 3 minutes. Pour the orange juice into a measuring jug with the reserved marinade, then make up to 450 ml (¾ pint) with water. Pour over the mushrooms and bring to the boil. Cover the pan and simmer gently for about 10 minutes.

Meanwhile cook the chops under a preheated grill for 6-8 minutes on each side.

Blend the cornflour with a little water until smooth, then stir into the mushroom mixture. Bring to the boil, stirring continuously, then season the sauce to taste. Serve with the chops. Note: This sauce is equally delicious served with duck. **Serves 4**

Top right: Honey-glazed pork and mushrooms; Lamb with mushroom and orange sauce (bottom left).

INGREDIENTS

2 pork loin chops
30 ml (2 tbsp) set honey
10 ml (2 tsp) wholegrain mustard
150 g (5 oz) button mushrooms
GARNISH
chopped parsley

4-6 lamb loin chops
MARINADE
juice of 1 large orange
20 ml (4 tsp) chopped fresh mint
10 ml (2 tsp) cider vinegar
10 ml (2 tsp) olive oil
SAUCE
30 ml (2 tbsp) oil
1 small onion, finely chopped
2 cloves garlic, crushed
225 g (8 oz) chestnut mushrooms, sliced
juice of 2 oranges
20-25 ml (4-5 tsp) cornflour

Stir-fried chicken, mushrooms and prawns

Heat the oil in a wok or large frying pan, stir in the celery and onion. Cover and cook over a gentle heat for 3 minutes. Stir in the garlic, mushrooms, chicken, prawns and seasoning. Cover and continue cooking for 8-10 minutes, stirring occasionally. Stir in the lemon juice. Serve garnished with parsley and lemon slices. **Serves 4**

INGREDIENTS

30 ml (2 tbsp) oil
3 sticks celery, finely chopped
1 large onion, sliced lengthways
2 cloves garlic, crushed
350 g (12 oz) open cup mushrooms
275 g (10 oz) chicken breast, cut into strips
125 g (4 oz) peeled cooked prawns
30 ml (2 tbsp) lemon juice

Stir-fried chilli beef

Add water to the orange juice to make 250 ml (8 fl oz). Put the steak in a mixing bowl with the diluted orange juice, chillies and lemon juice. Mix well, cover and leave to marinate for at least 1 hour. Drain the steak, reserving the juices.

Heat the oil in a wok or large frying pan and stir in the steak and onion. Cover and cook for 3 minutes. Stir in the beans, red pepper and mushrooms. Cover and cook for 3 minutes. Stir in the reserved marinade. Bring to the boil, then stir in the peanut butter and seasoning and cook until the sauce thickens. Serve garnished with fresh herbs. **Serves 4**

575 g (1¼ lb) rump or sirloin steak, cut into thin strips
juice of 2 oranges
1-2 dried red chillies, crushed
30 ml (2 tbsp) lemon juice
30 ml (2 tbsp) oil
1 large onion, sliced into wedges
175 g (6 oz) broad beans
1 red pepper, seeded and cut into thin strips
350 g (12 oz) closed cup mushrooms, thickly sliced
60 ml (4 tbsp) peanut butter

Spicy stir-fried kidneys

Make criss-cross cuts in a lattice pattern halfway through the thickness of each kidney. Heat the oil in a wok. Add the kidneys and potatoes, cover and cook for 5 minutes. Add the carrots and courgettes, cover and cook for 5 minutes. Stir in the remaining ingredients, cover and cook for a further 20 minutes, stirring occasionally. **Serves 4**

5-6 lambs' kidneys, halved and cored
30 ml (2 tbsp) oil
350 g (12 oz) new potatoes, quartered
175 g (6 oz) new carrots, thinly sliced
225 g (8 oz) courgettes, thinly sliced
225 g (8 oz) chestnut mushrooms, sliced
1.25-2.5 ml (¼-½ tsp) hot chilli powder
5 ml (1 tsp) turmeric
5 ml (1 tsp) ground coriander
60 ml (4 tbsp) water

Right: Stir-fried chilli beef.

Fish crumble

Remove the skin from the smoked cod fillet and cut the fish into large cubes.

Heat the oil and cook the leeks and carrots for 2 minutes. Add the mushrooms and cook for 2 minutes. Stir in the flour and cook for a minute. Remove from the heat and stir in the milk gradually. Return to the heat and bring to the boil, stirring. Stir in three-quarters of the cheese and set aside.

Arrange the fish in a 1 litre (1¾ pint) ovenproof dish, then cover with the sauce. Rub the butter into the oatflakes, stir in the the remaining cheese, then sprinkle over the fish and sauce. Bake in a preheated 190°C (375°F/gas mark 5) oven for about 30 minutes. **Serves 4**

INGREDIENTS

450 g (1 lb) smoked cod fillet
30 ml (2 tbsp) oil
175 g (6 oz) leeks, sliced
2 carrots, diced
350 g (12 oz) closed cup mushrooms, thickly sliced
45 ml (3 tbsp) plain flour
250 ml (8 fl oz) milk
125 g (4 oz) Double Gloucester cheese, grated
25 g (1 oz) butter
25 g (1 oz) medium oatflakes

Mushroom-stuffed chicken

Melt the butter and cook the onion and mushrooms for 3 minutes. Stir in the garlic and cook for 30 seconds. Turn into a mixing bowl with the lime rind and juice, rice and seasoning. Leave to cool. Meanwhile, wipe the chicken all over with absorbent kitchen paper. Then, beginning at the neck end, insert your hands very carefully between the skin and the breast of the bird and ease the skin away from the breast slowly.

Use about three-quarters of the stuffing to form an even layer between the skin and the flesh of the chicken. Use the remainder to fill the neck end. Secure the neck flap with skewers or string. Weigh the stuffed chicken and calculate the cooking time. Brush the chicken lightly with oil and season. Put into a roasting tin and bake in a preheated 190°C (375°F/gas mark 5) oven for 20 minutes per 450 g (1 lb) plus 20 minutes. If the stuffing appears to be overbrowning, cover the chicken with a sheet of wet greaseproof paper. **Serves 4-6**

Right: Mushroom-stuffed chicken.

1.6 kg (3½ lb) chicken
oil

STUFFING

25 g (1 oz) butter
1 small onion, finely chopped
175 g (6 oz) closed cup mushrooms, very finely chopped
1 clove garlic, crushed
grated rind and juice of ½ lime
50 g (2 oz) jasmine rice, cooked and drained

NOTE

The stuffing ingredients can be doubled to stuff a 4.5 kg (10 lb) turkey

Light Meals and Suppers

One of the best ways to make a quick meal is with mushrooms. Mushrooms on toast, stuffed mushrooms or toasted bacon and mushroom sandwiches are all firm favourites. Make a pasta sauce or a pizza more interesting with sliced mushrooms. These recipes are ideal for people with limited cooking facilities in, say, a holiday cottage or caravan.

Mushrooms with pasta quills

Put the mushrooms, spring onions and thyme into a large mixing bowl and pour over the grape juice. Mix well, cover and chill for about 3 hours, stirring occasionally. Stir in the grapes and drained, cooled pasta just before serving. **Serves 4**

INGREDIENTS

350 g (12 oz) button mushrooms
6 large spring onions, chopped
15 ml (1 tbsp) chopped fresh thyme
200 ml (7 fl oz) grape juice
225 g (8 oz) white seedless grapes, halved
175 g (6 oz) cooked pasta quills

Tagliatelle with mushrooms and garlic cheese

Heat the oil and butter together in a saucepan, add the mushrooms and garlic, cover and cook gently for about 5 minutes. Stir in the spinach and cook for a minute. Stir in the ricotta, white wine and seasoning and cook gently for about 3 minutes. Add the tagliatelle carefully and fold the sauce through the pasta. Serve immediately, garnished with parsley. **Serves 4**

30 ml (2 tbsp) oil
15 g (½ oz) butter
350 g (12 oz) button mushrooms, halved
2 cloves garlic, crushed
225 g (8 oz) frozen chopped spinach, thawed
250 g (9 oz) ricotta cheese
75 ml (5 tbsp) white wine
225 g (8 oz) fresh tagliatelle, cooked and drained
GARNISH
parsley

Right: Mushrooms with pasta quills.

Mushrooms on toast

Trim the mushroom stalks (use for soup or stock). Preheat the grill. Melt the butter in a saucepan (or in a microwave). Put the mushrooms, cap side up, on the grill rack and brush with half the butter. Grill for 2 minutes. Turn the mushrooms over, brush with the remaining butter and grill for a further 2 minutes. Serve on toast. If liked, season with black pepper, lemon juice, Worcestershire sauce or sherry. (Alternatively, cook in the microwave on High for 2 minutes.) **Serves 2**

INGREDIENTS

225 g (8 oz) open cup mushrooms
25 g (1 oz) butter
2 slices toast
black pepper (optional)
lemon juice (optional)
Worcestershire sauce or sherry (optional)

Toasted bacon and mushroom sandwich

Preheat a sandwich toaster. Oil a frying pan lightly, add the bacon and cook gently for 3 minutes until the fat begins to run. Add the mushrooms and cook briskly until the bacon is crisp. Season with black pepper. If liked, add the beaten egg and cook for 1 minute. Butter the bread on one side only. Place two slices of the bread in the toaster, butter side down, and spoon the mushroom mixture on top. Cover with the remaining bread, butter side up, and cook until brown. **Makes 2 sandwiches**

5 ml (1 tsp) oil
2 rashers streaky bacon, chopped
125 g (4 oz) open cup mushrooms, sliced
black pepper
1 beaten egg (optional)
butter
4 slices bread

Devilled mushrooms

Mix the fromage frais, Worcestershire sauce and mustard together in a saucepan. Stir in the mushrooms and cook over a gentle heat for about 6 minutes. Do not allow the mixture to boil. Serve with triangles of toast. **Serves 4**

150 g (5 oz) very low-fat natural fromage frais
10 ml (2 tsp) Worcestershire sauce
10 ml (2 tsp) wholegrain mustard
225 g (8 oz) open cup mushrooms, sliced
TO SERVE
triangles of toast

Top left: Toasted bacon and mushroom sandwich; Devilled mushrooms (top right); Mushrooms on toast (bottom).

Stuffed mushrooms

INGREDIENTS

50 g (2 oz) butter
125 g (4 oz) fresh chicken fillet, minced
1 small onion, minced
25 g (1 oz) granary bread, crumbed
15 ml (1 tbsp) chopped mixed fresh herbs
4 large open mushrooms

Melt half the butter and cook the chicken and onion for about 5 minutes, stirring occasionally. Leave to cool, then stir in the breadcrumbs, herbs and seasoning. Mix well and divide between the mushrooms. Arrange the mushrooms in a roasting tin and dot with the remaining butter. Bake in a preheated 190°C (375°F/gas mark 5) oven for 20-25 minutes. **Serves 2**

Souffléd omelette

2 eggs, separated
15 ml (1 tbsp) milk
5 ml (1 tsp) chopped fresh thyme
FILLING
15 ml (1 tbsp) oil
125 g (4 oz) chestnut mushrooms, sliced
5 ml (1 tsp) plain flour
2.5 ml (½ tsp) paprika
45 ml (3 tbsp) milk
5 ml (1 tsp) tomato purée

To make the filling, heat the oil and cook the mushrooms gently for about 4 minutes, stirring occasionally. Stir in the flour and paprika and cook for a minute. Add the remaining ingredients gradually and bring to the boil, stirring continuously, then cook over a very gentle heat whilst making the omelette.

Beat the egg yolks, milk and thyme together. Whisk the egg whites, then fold into the yolk mixture. Make the omelette as usual, then place the pan under a preheated grill and cook until golden. Slide the omelette on to a warm plate. Spoon the filling on to one half of the omelette, then flip over. **Serves 1**

Mushroom gnocchi

75 g (3 oz) butter
350 g (12 oz) closed cup mushrooms, very finely chopped
225 g (8 oz) curd cheese
40 g (1½ oz) Parmesan cheese, grated
2 eggs, beaten
50 g (2 oz) plain flour
freshly grated nutmeg
1 large clove garlic, crushed
GARNISH
chopped parsley

Melt 25 g (1 oz) of the butter and fry the mushrooms for 3 minutes. Drain, then beat in the cheeses, beaten egg, flour, nutmeg and seasoning. Leave until cold. With well-floured hands, shape large spoonfuls of the mixture into balls. Lower into a large pan of simmering water and cook for 4 minutes. Drain. Keep hot in a warm oven. Sauté the garlic in the remaining butter for 30 seconds. Pour over the gnocchi and sprinkle with parsley. **Serves 4**

Right: Stuffed mushrooms.

Mushroom pizza

Make up the pizza base according to the packet instructions. Roll out the dough to a 25 cm (10 inch) circle and put on a greased baking sheet. Heat the oil in a large pan and stir-fry the mushrooms quickly for 1 minute to seal in the juices. Add the garlic and basil, and stir-fry for a further minute. Spoon the mushrooms over the pizza base, season and sprinkle the grated mozzarella on top. Bake in a preheated 220°C (425°F/gas mark 7) oven for 20 minutes. **Serves 2**

INGREDIENTS

150 g (5 oz) pizza base mix
30 ml (2 tbsp) oil
350 g (12 oz) chestnut mushrooms, thickly sliced
1 clove garlic, chopped
4 fresh basil leaves, chopped
75 g (3 oz) mozzarella cheese, grated

Mushrooms in garlic butter

Fry the mushrooms lightly in hot oil for about 20 seconds, then drain well on absorbent kitchen paper. Mix the butter, garlic, herbs, seasoning and lemon juice together. Arrange the mushrooms, stalk side uppermost, in a shallow baking tin. Spoon a little of the garlic butter into each mushroom, then press some breadcrumbs lightly on top. Cook under a medium grill for about 5 minutes until the breadcrumbs are golden brown. Serve on small heated plates. Pour over any remaining melted garlic butter and serve with crusty bread. **Serves 4**

450 g (1 lb) open cup mushrooms
oil for frying
50 g (2 oz) unsalted butter, softened
2-3 cloves garlic, crushed
30 ml (2 tbsp) chopped fresh herbs
10 ml (2 tsp) lemon juice
50 g (2 oz) fresh breadcrumbs

Top right: Mushroom pizza; Mushrooms in garlic butter (bottom).

Mushroom and seafood fried rice

Heat the oil in a large frying pan and cook the onion and celery for about 2 minutes. Stir in the Basmati rice and cook for a minute, then stir in the curry powder and mushrooms and cook for a further minute. Stir in the water and bring to the boil. Simmer gently for 5 minutes. Add the prawns, mixed peanuts and raisins and drained sweetcorn, and cook for a further 4 minutes. Stir in the tuna carefully with seasoning to taste and cook for a minute or until the rice is tender and the water absorbed. Garnish with lemon wedges. **Serves 4**

Smoked cod flan

Heat the oil and cook the spring onions and mushrooms gently. Spoon half into the flan case, lay the fish on top and cover with the remaining mushrooms. Beat the egg and milk together and pour over the fish. Bake in a preheated 180°C (350°F/gas mark 4) oven for 40-45 minutes. Garnish with lemon slices. **Serves 4**

Salami risotto

Heat the oil and cook the mushrooms and spring onions for about 3 minutes. Add the rice and spices, and cook for another minute. Add 150 ml (¼ pint) of the stock and simmer gently, stirring occasionally, until all the liquid has been absorbed. Add a further 150 ml (¼ pint) of the stock and repeat as before. Add the remaining stock and other ingredients. Simmer gently, stirring occasionally, until the stock has been absorbed and the rice is cooked. **Serves 4**

Right: Mushroom and seafood fried rice.

INGREDIENTS

30 ml (2 tbsp) oil
1 onion, finely chopped
2 sticks celery, chopped
225 g (8 oz) Basmati rice
15 ml (1 tbsp) hot curry powder
350 g (12 oz) closed cup mushrooms, thickly sliced
600 ml (1 pint) water
125 g (4 oz) frozen peeled cooked prawns
125 g (4 oz) mixed peanuts and raisins
200 g (7 oz) can sweetcorn kernels
200 g (7 oz) can tuna, drained

30 ml (2 tbsp) oil
50 g (2 oz) spring onions, finely chopped
225 g (8 oz) closed cup mushrooms, thinly sliced
18 cm (7 inch) baked short crust flan case
175 g (6 oz) smoked cod fillet, cooked, skinned and flaked
1 egg (size 4), beaten
90 ml (6 tbsp) milk

15 ml (1 tbsp) oil
450 g (1 lb) closed cup mushrooms
1 bunch spring onions, chopped
175 g (6 oz) risotto rice
5 ml (1 tsp) ground turmeric
5 ml (1 tsp) ground coriander
450 ml (¾ pint) chicken stock
200 g (7 oz) can sweetcorn with peppers, drained
75 g (3 oz) salami, cut into thin strips

Entertaining

Mushrooms grow in a variety of attractive shapes and each has its own special flavour and texture. More cultivated speciality mushrooms are coming into our shops, particularly chestnut, oyster and shiitake mushrooms. Buy some of these varieties and mix them with small button mushrooms. Here are some exotic recipes to impress your guests.

Sauté of speciality mushrooms

INGREDIENTS

SPAETZLI

150 g (5 oz) plain flour
2 eggs (size 4)
1.25 ml (¼ tsp) grated nutmeg
salt and pepper
45 ml (3 tbsp) olive oil

SAUTE

675 g (1½ lb) mixed button, oyster and shiitake mushrooms
20 ml (4 tsp) olive oil
4 shallots, finely chopped
15 ml (1 tbsp) frangelico or amaretto liqueur
150 ml (¼ pint) mushroom stock (see method)
150 ml (¼ pint) veal or chicken stock
15 ml (1 tbsp) chopped fresh chervil
15 ml (1 tbsp) chopped parsley
25 g (1 oz) unsalted butter

TO SERVE

rocket salad dressed with balsamico vinaigrette

NOTE

Cooked pasta can be used as an alternative to the spaetzli.

To make the spaetzli, put all the ingredients except 30 ml (2 tbsp) of the oil into a bowl and beat well. Freeze for 1 hour. Then scrape the dough on to a coarse grater, being careful that the dough forms into large shreds and not lumps. Use a little extra flour if necessary. Plunge the spaetzli into boiling salted water for 1 minute. Drain and cover with cold water to cool. Strain the spaetzli and pat dry with absorbent kitchen paper. Heat the remaining olive oil in a large non-stick pan and sauté the spaetzli until golden brown. Drain on absorbent kitchen paper and keep warm while preparing the sauté.

Trim the stalks from the mushrooms and put into a saucepan with 150 ml (¼ pint) water. Bring to the boil and simmer for a few minutes. Strain off the liquid and use for mushroom stock.

Heat the oil in the large non-stick pan until very hot. Sauté the mushrooms for 1 minute. Add the shallots and continue to sauté. Pour in the liqueur, add the mushroom stock and cook until the quantity of liquid is reduced by half; then add the veal stock and again cook until the quantity of liquid is reduced by half. Stir in the herbs and butter. Season to taste. Add the spaetzli and serve immediately with a dressed rocket salad. **Serves 4**

Right: Sauté of speciality mushrooms.

Mushroom choux puffs

Melt the margarine slowly in the water. Bring to the boil, then stir in the flour and salt quickly. Beat to a smooth ball. Leave to cool, then beat in the eggs and mustard gradually until smooth and glossy. Stir in the mushrooms. Place 24 spoonfuls of the mixture on to a lightly greased baking sheet. Bake in a preheated 200°C (400°F/gas mark 6) oven for 15 minutes, then reduce the oven temperature to 180°C (350°F/gas mark 4) and cook for a further 15-20 minutes. Serve hot, using cocktail sticks. **Makes 24**

Golden mushroom and cod nuggets

Blend the soured cream and horseradish sauce together, then chill. Put the cod and mushrooms in a food processor and blend until fairly smooth. Add the parsley and seasoning. Shape into 24 balls, then chill for at least 1 hour.

Mix the breadcrumbs and hazelnuts together. Dip the balls into the egg, then coat in the breadcrumb mixture. Chill until ready to fry in hot oil until golden brown. Drain, then serve hot with the horseradish sauce. Garnish with coriander. **Makes 24**

Mushroom dip with crudités

Put all the ingredients in a food processor and blend until fairly smooth. Turn into a serving dish. Cover and chill for about 1 hour. Serve surrounded by prepared salad vegetables. **Serves 10**

Top, centre: Mushroom dip with crudités; Golden mushroom and cod nuggets (left); Mushroom choux puffs (bottom, right).

INGREDIENTS

50 g (2 oz) margarine
125 ml (4 fl oz) water
65 g (2½ oz) strong plain flour
pinch of salt
2 eggs (size 4), beaten
5-10 ml (1-2 tsp) Dijon mustard
125 g (4 oz) chestnut mushrooms, roughly chopped

150 ml (¼ pint) soured cream
30 ml (2 tbsp) horseradish sauce
225 g (8 oz) cod fillet, skinned and chopped
225 g (8 oz) closed cup mushrooms, chopped
45 ml (3 tbsp) chopped parsley
75 g (3 oz) wholemeal breadcrumbs
60 ml (4 tbsp) chopped hazelnuts
1 egg, beaten
oil for deep frying
GARNISH
coriander

2 sticks celery, very finely chopped
225 g (8 oz) button mushrooms, very finely chopped
125 g (4 oz) low-fat fromage frais with garlic and parsley
60 ml (4 tbsp) natural yogurt
TO SERVE
a selection of fresh salad vegetables

Stilton and mushroom vol-au-vent

Cook the vol-au-vent cases according to the packet instructions. Meanwhile, heat the oil and cook the celery and mushrooms for 3 minutes. Stir in the flour and cook for a minute. Stir in the milk gradually and bring to the boil, stirring continuously. Add the apple and cook for a minute. Add the Stilton and seasoning, stirring until the cheese has melted. Fill the vol-au-vent cases with the sauce and serve. **Makes 16**

INGREDIENTS

16 frozen individual vol-au-vent cases
45 ml (3 tbsp) oil
1 stick celery, finely chopped
225 g (8 oz) button mushrooms, sliced
45 ml (3 tbsp) plain flour
300 ml (½ pint) milk
1 apple, peeled, cored and diced
175 g (6 oz) Stilton cheese, grated

Duck and mushroom special

Prepare the mushrooms by making a series of curved cuts with a sharp knife from the top of the mushroom to the base. Remove a narrow strip along each cut.

Discard the excess fat from the duck breasts. Heat the oil, then cook the duck, skin side up, over a high heat until just browned. Transfer to a rack placed in a roasting tin. Cook the duck in a preheated 230°C (450°F/gas mark 8) oven for 6-8 minutes, then transfer to a warmed plate and set aside.

Heat the oil remaining in the roasting tin and cook the mushrooms and peppercorns for about 3 minutes. Remove the mushrooms with a slotted spoon and keep warm. Stir in the flour and cook for 1 minute. Stir in the cognac, stock and seasoning gradually. Bring to the boil, stirring, and reduce the quantity by half. Then stir in the cream gradually, do not allow it to boil.

Remove the skin from the duck breasts quickly and discard. Slice the duck thinly, then re-shape into breasts. Spoon the sauce on to warmed plates. Arrange the duck and mushrooms on the sauce. Garnish with coriander. **Serves 2**

275 g (10 oz) closed cup mushrooms, stalks trimmed
2 large duck breasts
15 ml (1 tbsp) oil
15 g (½ oz) fresh green peppercorns
10 ml (2 tsp) plain flour
75 ml (5 tbsp) cognac
200 ml (7 fl oz) light stock
75 ml (5 tbsp) single cream
GARNISH
sprig of coriander

Right: Duck and mushroom special.

Golden mushroom and tomato tart

Place a 25 cm (10 inch) loose-bottomed fluted flan tin on a baking sheet. Brush with a little butter. Unfold the pastry, brush one sheet with butter, fold in half and place in the flan tin so that it extends over the sides. Brush the top with butter. Repeat with 5 more sheets, placing them in the flan tin so that the corners project like the spokes of a wheel.

Arrange the mushrooms, tomatoes, thyme and cheese in layers on top of pastry. Bring the pastry edges over towards the centre. Brush the remaining sheets of pastry with butter, fold in half, then place on top of the tart, tucking down the edges. Brush the top with butter. Bake in a preheated 190°C (375°F/gas mark 5) oven for about 25 minutes until golden brown. **Serves 4**

INGREDIENTS

65 g (2½ oz) butter, melted
8 sheets filo pastry
350 g (12 oz) closed cup mushrooms, sliced
2 beefsteak tomatoes, peeled, seeded and chopped
10 ml (2 tsp) chopped fresh thyme
175 g (6 oz) Cheddar cheese, grated

Mille feuille of mushrooms

Thaw the pastry according to the instructions on the packet. Cut into four triangles. Score a smaller triangle within each triangle. Brush with egg wash and bake in a preheated 200°C (400°F/gas mark 6) oven for 10 minutes. Meanwhile, heat the calvados in a large shallow pan. Add the mushrooms and flambé. Remove the mushrooms and keep warm. Boil the remaining calvados until reduced by half and reserve. In a separate pan, cook the shallot, garlic and bacon for 3 minutes. Add the mustard, cream, pepper and reserved calvados. Heat gently but do not boil. Stir in the butter in small knobs to thicken the sauce.

Remove the inner triangle from each pastry case carefully, fill with the cooked mushrooms and pour a little sauce over them. Replace the 'lids'. Pour the remaining sauce around the pastry cases. Garnish with fried apple slices. **Makes 4**

one 20 cm (8 inch) square sheet frozen puff pastry (or roll out puff pastry to make 20 cm (8 inch) square, 5mm (¼ inch) thick)
beaten egg and milk
125 ml (4 fl oz) calvados
350 g (12 oz) mixed button, oyster and shiitake mushrooms
1 shallot, finely chopped
1 clove garlic, finely chopped
1 rasher bacon, finely chopped
5 ml (1 tsp) Dijon mustard
150 ml (¼ pint) double cream
pinch of black pepper
25 g (1 oz) unsalted butter

GARNISH

fried apple slices

Right: Golden mushroom and tomato tart.

Charlotte of mushrooms and salmon with lentils

Cook the lentils according to the instructions on the packet. Meanwhile, mix together the minced salmon, salt and egg white. Chill. Take half the given quantity of shiitake mushrooms, selecting the larger ones, and cut the mushrooms horizontally across the caps. Heat half the Madeira and blanch the mushroom caps. Remove with a slotted spoon. Chop the leftover pieces of shiitake mushrooms, discarding the stalks, and blanch in the same Madeira. Boil until the quantity of liquid is reduced by half.

Line four dariole moulds or ramekins with the shiitake mushroom caps. Mix 125 ml (4 fl oz) of the cream into the chilled salmon. Spoon some of the salmon into the moulds, leaving a well in the centre. Add a dash of cream to the chopped cooked shiitake mushrooms and reduce until thick. Season. Fill the moulds with the cooked mushrooms and cover with the remaining salmon mixture. Put the moulds in a roasting tin filled with hot water and cook in a preheated 160°C (325°F/gas mark 3) oven for 10-15 minutes.

Meanwhile, pour the stock, wine and the remaining Madeira into a saucepan and reduce the quantity of liquid by three-quarters. Add the remaining cream and season to taste. Cut the remaining shiitake mushrooms into quarters, and discard the stalks. Mix with the oyster mushrooms and poach gently in the Madeira sauce until cooked.

Spoon a pile of cooked lentils on to each plate. Turn out the salmon moulds beside the lentils. Pour the Madeira sauce around the salmon and garnish with asparagus spears. **Serves 4**

INGREDIENTS

75 g (3 oz) green lentils
225 g (8 oz) fresh salmon, minced
pinch of salt
1 egg white, beaten
225 g (8 oz) shiitake or large open mushrooms
200 ml (7 fl oz) Madeira
200 ml (7 fl oz) double cream
150 ml (¼ pint) chicken stock
50 ml (2 fl oz) white wine
125 g (4 oz) oyster mushrooms

GARNISH

cooked asparagus spears

Right: Charlotte of mushrooms and salmon with lentils.

Vegetarian Recipes

Many of the other recipes in this book are also suitable for vegetarians and vegans, but this chapter is specifically for them. Today, many families or groups have just one vegetarian in their midst and some people find it difficult to cook for them. The recipes will help those non-vegetarians who want to cook a dish that is acceptable to both meat-eaters and vegetarians.

Stir-fried oyster mushrooms

INGREDIENTS

30 ml (2 tbsp) sesame seed oil
175 g (6 oz) carrots, cut into strips
1 green pepper, seeded and cubed
225 g (8 oz) oyster mushrooms, sliced
225 g (8 oz) can sliced bamboo shoots, drained
30 ml (2 tbsp) light soy sauce
30 ml (2 tbsp) hoi sin sauce
30 ml (2 tbsp) stock

Heat the oil in a wok or large frying pan. Stir in the carrot and green pepper, cover and cook for 1 minute. Stir in the mushrooms, cover and cook for 2 minutes, stirring occasionally. Add the bamboo shoots, then stir in the remaining ingredients gradually. Bring to the boil and simmer for 1 minute; then serve garnished with spring onion curls. **Serves 4**

Chinese stir-fry

30 ml (2 tbsp) sesame oil
125 g (4 oz) baby corn cobs
1 large red pepper, seeded and cut into narrow strips
150 g (5 oz) mange tout, topped and tailed
1 bunch spring onions, cut into 5 cm (2 inch) lengths
275 g (10 oz) button mushrooms, halved
2.5 cm (1 inch) piece of fresh ginger, grated
5 ml (1 tsp) ground ginger
60 ml (4 tbsp) soy sauce
15 ml (1 tbsp) set honey
45 ml (3 tbsp) tomato ketchup
225 g (8 oz) fresh bean sprouts
15 ml (1 tbsp) cornflour

Heat the oil in a wok. Stir in the baby corn, red pepper and mange tout. Cover and cook for 2 minutes. Stir in the spring onions, mushrooms and grated ginger, and cook for another minute. Stir in the ground ginger and cook for a few seconds; then stir in the soy sauce, honey and tomato ketchup. Bring to the boil, cover and cook gently for about 3 minutes. Stir in the bean sprouts, and cook gently for a further 2 minutes. Blend the cornflour with a little water until smooth, then stir into the vegetables. Bring to the boil and serve immediately. **Serves 4**

Right: Chinese stir-fry.

Mushroom flan

Roll out the pastry and use to line a deep 20 cm (8 inch) loose-bottomed flan tin. Prick the base all over very thoroughly with a fork. Line with foil or greaseproof paper and fill with old dried beans. Bake in a preheated 200°C (400°F/gas mark 6) oven for 15 minutes. Remove the beans and foil or paper. Reduce the oven temperature to 190°C (375°F/gas mark 5).

Meanwhile, heat the margarine and oil in a pan and fry the onion gently for 2-3 minutes. Do not allow it to brown. Add the mushrooms, herbs and seasoning, and continue to fry gently for about 5 minutes. Beat in the cream and eggs and pour the mixture into the par-baked pastry case. Continue cooking for 35-40 minutes. Serve with a salad. **Serves 4-6**

INGREDIENTS

200 g (7 oz) shortcrust pastry
25 g (1 oz) margarine
10 ml (2 tsp) cooking oil
1 large onion, sliced
450 g (1 lb) chestnut mushrooms, sliced
15 ml (1 tbsp) chopped parsley
1.25 ml (1/4 tsp) garlic salt (optional)
150 ml (1/4 pint) double cream
2 eggs (size 4), beaten

Creamy mushroom and parsnip bake

Blend the parsnips in a food processor until smooth. Heat 10 ml (2 tsp) of the oil and brown the onion quickly. Turn into the processor with the parsnips, coriander, eggs, cream and seasoning, and blend until fairly smooth.

Heat the remaining oil and cook the mushrooms and cumin seeds for 5 minutes. Drain. Spread the margarine over the bread, and cut each slice into two triangles.

Oil four 300 ml (½ pint) ovenproof dishes lightly. Line each dish with four triangles of bread. Spoon in half the parsnip mixture, then half the mushrooms; repeat the layers. Bake in a preheated 190°C (375°F/gas mark 5) oven for about 30 minutes. Serve garnished with coriander. **Serves 4**

450 g (1 lb) parsnips, cooked and drained
40 ml (8 tsp) oil
1 onion, roughly chopped
30 ml (2 tbsp) chopped fresh coriander
2 eggs (size 4), beaten
45 ml (3 tbsp) double cream
275 g (10 oz) open cup mushrooms, sliced
5 ml (1 tsp) cumin seeds
margarine
8 slices brown bread, crusts removed
GARNISH
sprigs of fresh coriander

Top right: Mushroom flan; Creamy mushroom and parsnip bake (centre and bottom).

Tossed mixed salad with oranges

Tear the lettuce into small pieces and put into a salad bowl with the watercress, oranges, green pepper, olives and mushrooms. Put the avocado in a bowl with the lemon juice and mix together before spooning into the mushroom mixture, then toss together. **Serves 4**

Layered terrine

To make the carrot layer, melt the margarine and cook the garlic until soft, then beat into the carrot purée with the thyme, bread-crumbs and egg. Set aside. Mix all the ingredients for the mush-room layer together; then set aside. Pick over the spinach leaves and discard any thick stalks and yellow leaves. Wash and drain the spinach, then cook in a covered saucepan over a gentle heat for about 3 minutes. Squeeze out as much moisture as possible, then finely chop. Melt the margarine and cook the onion until soft. Add to the spinach with the egg and a little grated nutmeg.

Oil a 1.1 litre (2 pint) terrine dish lightly. Spoon the carrot mixture into the base and spread evenly. Spoon in the mush-room mixture, then the spinach mixture and spread evenly. Cover with a lightly oiled sheet of foil. Place in a roasting tin half-filled with hot water. Bake in a preheated 170°C (325°F/gas mark 3) oven for about 1 hour 10 minutes or until the top is firm to the touch. Leave to cool.

Dissolve the aspic jelly powder in the lemon juice and 30 ml (2 tbsp) cold water in a small bowl over a pan of hot water or in a microwave. Make up to 300 ml (½ pint) with cold water. Pour a very thin layer on top of the spinach. Chill to set. Decorate with sliced mushrooms, then carefully spoon a little more aspic over the top. Chill until set, then carefully spoon a little more aspic over the top. Again chill until set. **Serves 6-8**

Top left: Tossed mixed salad with oranges; Layered terrine (top right and bottom).

INGREDIENTS

1 lollo rosso lettuce
1 bunch watercress
2 oranges, peeled, halved and sliced
1 green pepper, seeded and cut into strips
12 stoned black olives, halved
225 g (8 oz) button mushrooms
2 avocados, peeled, stoned and chopped
30 ml (2 tbsp) lemon juice

CARROT LAYER
15 g (½ oz) margarine
2 cloves garlic, crushed
350 g (12 oz) carrots, cooked, drained and mashed to a purée
10 ml (2 tsp) chopped fresh thyme
25 g (1 oz) fresh wholemeal breadcrumbs
1 egg (size 4) beaten

MUSHROOM LAYER
225 g (8 oz) closed cup mushrooms, very finely chopped
60 ml (4 tbsp) soured cream
25 g (1 oz) fresh wholemeal breadcrumbs

SPINACH LAYER
450 g (1 lb) fresh spinach
15 g (½ oz) margarine
1 onion, very finely chopped
1 egg (size 4), beaten
freshly grated nutmeg

ASPIC GLAZE
15 ml (1 tbsp) aspic jelly powder
15 ml (1 tbsp) lemon juice

DECORATION
raw button mushrooms, sliced

Nutty mushroom and Stilton pie

To make the filling, heat the oil and fry the celery and spring onions lightly for about 3 minutes. Stir in the mushrooms and cook for about 5 minutes. Stir in the flour and cook for a minute. Remove from the heat and stir in the water gradually. Return to the heat and bring to the boil, stirring. Add seasoning and the hazelnuts, then leave to cool.

To make the pastry, put the flour and salt into a mixing bowl. Rub in the margarine, and add enough water to form a not too stiff dough. Roll out just over half the pastry, and use to line a 25 cm (10 inch) loose-bottomed flan ring. Moisten the pastry edges with water. Turn the cold mushroom mixture into the flan case, then sprinkle the cheese over the top. Roll out the remaining pastry, and use to cover the pie, sealing the edges well. Garnish with pastry leaves cut from the trimmings. Brush with egg or milk, and bake in a preheated 200°C (400°F/gas mark 6) oven for 40 minutes. **Serves 6**

INGREDIENTS

30 ml (2 tbsp) vegetable oil
3 sticks celery, chopped
1 bunch spring onions, chopped
250 g (9 oz) large open mushrooms, thickly sliced
45 ml (3 tbsp) plain flour
300 ml (½ pint) water
25 g (1 oz) hazelnuts, chopped
75 g (3 oz) Stilton cheese, grated
beaten egg or milk

PASTRY

225 g (8 oz) plain and wholemeal flour in equal quantities
pinch of salt
125 g (4 oz) margarine

Mushroom, orange and pistachio nut roast

Heat the oil and cook the leeks until soft. Turn into a mixing bowl with the remaining ingredients and mix well. Turn the mixture into a lightly oiled ovenproof dish. Cover with oiled foil, then bake in a preheated 190°C (375°F/gas mark 5) oven for about 45 minutes. Serve hot or cold, garnished with sliced oranges. **Serves 8**

15 ml (1 tbsp) oil
225 g (8 oz) leeks, very finely chopped
125 g (4 oz) pistachios, very finely chopped
125 g (4 oz) hazelnuts, very finely chopped
125 g (4 oz) almonds, very finely chopped
grated rind of 1 orange
50 g (2 oz) fresh breadcrumbs
225 g (8 oz) closed cup mushrooms, very finely chopped
2 eggs (size 4), beaten

GARNISH

sliced oranges

Top: Nutty mushroom and Stilton pie; Mushroom, orange and pistachio nut roast (bottom right, in dish).

Winter mushroom casserole

Heat the oil and cook the spring onions for 2 minutes. Stir in the turnips, carrots, celery and mushrooms, and cook for about 3 minutes. Stir in the flour and cook for a minute. Remove from the heat and stir in the tomatoes and stock gradually. Return to the heat and bring to the boil, stirring. Stir in the remaining ingredients, then simmer gently for about 15 minutes. Garnish with parsley and serve with chunks of garlic bread. **Serves 4**

Mushroom and ginger wine salad

Mix the mushrooms, melon, tomatoes and spring onion together. Add the ginger wine, then cover and chill for at least 2 hours, stirring occasionally. **Serves 4-6**

Black-eyed bean Bourguignonne

Boil the beans rapidly for 10 minutes, then drain. Heat the oil and cook the onions quickly until brown. Add the carrots, then cook for 3 minutes. Stir in the beans with the wine, stock, tomato purée and herbs. Bring to the boil, cover and simmer gently for 50 minutes, adding the mushrooms after 30 minutes. Blend the cornflour with the water, then stir into the mixture. Boil for 1 minute, then season. **Serves 4**

Right: Black-eyed bean Bourguignonne.

INGREDIENTS

30 ml (2 tbsp) oil
1 bunch spring onions, cut into 5 cm (2 inch) lengths
275 g (10 oz) turnips, diced
2 carrots, diagonally sliced
3 sticks celery, diagonally sliced
350 g (12 oz) chestnut mushrooms
45 ml (3 tbsp) plain flour
400 g (14 oz) can chopped peeled tomatoes
350 ml (12 fl oz) vegetable stock
400 g (14 oz) can borlotti beans, drained
25 ml (5 tsp) hot pepper and lime sauce

350 g (12 oz) button mushrooms, halved
½ honeydew melon, seeded and cut into balls or cubes
4 tomatoes, peeled, seeded, then flesh cut into strips
1 large spring onion, very finely chopped
90 ml (6 tbsp) ginger wine

175 g (6 oz) black-eyed beans, soaked overnight and drained
30 ml (2 tbsp) oil
225 g (8 oz) button onions
225 g (8 oz) carrots, cut into large chunks
300 ml (½ pint) red wine
150 ml (¼ pint) vegetable stock
30 ml (2 tbsp) tomato purée
2 bay leaves
30 ml (2 tbsp) chopped parsley
225 g (8 oz) button mushrooms
15 ml (1 tbsp) cornflour
15 ml (1 tbsp) water

Outdoor Eating

Mushrooms are perfect for barbecues, picnics or lunches on the patio. Thread on to kebab skewers or wrap in foil to cook on a barbecue. Vegetarians in particular will love them – so often, a barbecue means sausages and steaks. If you want to relax on a summer weekend, make a chilled mousse or flan the day before so you are not tied to the kitchen.

Peppered bacon and mushroom kebabs

INGREDIENTS

2 small new potatoes
1 rasher back bacon
4 large closed cup mushrooms
oil
paprika
salt

Boil the potatoes until just tender, then drain and cool quickly to stop further cooking. Cut the bacon rasher in half and roll up both pieces. Thread the mushrooms, potatoes and bacon on to a kebab skewer. Brush with oil and keep cool for 1 hour, brushing with oil again before cooking. Brush with paprika, then with salt. Cook on a barbecue (or under a preheated grill) for 5 minutes, turning once. **Makes 1 kebab**

Pork and apple burgers

575 g (1¼ lb) lean pork, minced
1 small onion, very finely chopped
225 g (8 oz) open cup mushrooms, very finely chopped
50 g (2 oz) fresh wholemeal breadcrumbs
225 g (8 oz) cooking apples, peeled, cored and very finely chopped
1 egg (size 4), beaten
15 ml (1 tbsp) prepared mustard

Mix all the ingredients together in a bowl. With well-floured hands, shape the mixture into 8 burgers about 2.5 cm (1 inch) thick. Cover and chill until required.

Cook on a barbecue (or under a preheated grill) for about 10 minutes on each side, remembering that pork should be thoroughly cooked. **Makes 8 burgers**

Right: Pork and apple burgers.

Pickled mushrooms in oil

Pour the vinegar and water into a large enamelled saucepan. Add the cinnamon stick, cloves, peppercorns, bay leaves and salt. Bring to the boil. Add the mushrooms, return to the boil, then boil for 5 minutes. Spread a clean tea-towel on a work surface and cover with absorbent kitchen paper. Strain the mushrooms, then spread over the absorbent kitchen paper. Do not touch the mushrooms with your hands as they have now been sterilized. Cover lightly with absorbent kitchen paper. Allow the mushrooms to dry out for a few hours.

Spoon some of the mushrooms into sterilized jars without touching with your hands. Pour over enough oil to cover. Add more mushrooms and more oil to fill each jar. Seal tightly and store in a cool place for a month. Once opened, store in the refrigerator and eat within a short time. **Makes about 900 g (2 lb)**

INGREDIENTS

600 ml (1 pint) white wine vinegar
300 ml (½ pint) water
2.5 cm (1 inch) piece of cinnamon stick
10 ml (2 tsp) whole cloves
10 ml (2 tsp) black peppercorns
2 bay leaves
15 ml (1 tbsp) salt
900 g (2 lb) closed cup mushrooms, thickly sliced
250 ml (8 fl oz) olive oil

Chicken with mushroom and celery stuffing

To make the stuffing, mix all the ingredients together.

Stretch each bacon rasher over the back of a knife. Make a large slit down the side of each chicken breast, then gradually enlarge it to make a large pocket in which to insert the stuffing. Wrap a bacon rasher around each breast. Mix the glaze ingredients together. Cook the chicken breasts on a barbecue (or under a medium grill) for 5 minutes, then brush with some of the tomato glaze. Cook for a further 5 minutes. Turn the chicken breasts over and repeat, brushing with the remaining glaze after 5 minutes. **Serves 4**

4 large rashers back bacon, rinds removed
4 large boned chicken breasts

STUFFING

125 g (4 oz) large open mushrooms, very finely chopped
1 stick celery, very finely chopped
1 small bunch spring onions, very finely chopped
15 g (½ oz) fresh breadcrumbs
30 ml (2 tbsp) horseradish sauce

TOMATO GLAZE

30 ml (2 tbsp) tomato ketchup
15 ml (1 tbsp) soy sauce
15 ml (1 tbsp) oil

Right: Chicken with mushroom and celery stuffing.

Mushroom parcels

To make the filling, put the chickpeas in a food processor and blend for just 3-4 seconds to chop roughly. Turn into a bowl with the remaining filling ingredients and mix well. Spoon into the mushrooms and dot each with a little butter. Wrap the mushrooms individually in buttered foil. Cook the parcels on a barbecue for about 8 minutes (or cook, unwrapped, in a preheated 200°C (400°F/gas mark 6) oven for about 6 minutes). **Serves 4-6**

Vegetarian Brazil nut burgers

Heat the oil and cook the leek, courgettes and mushrooms for 5 minutes. Stir in the chilli powder and cook for 30 seconds. Add the remaining ingredients and mix well. Leave to cool; then shape into about 8 burgers. Cook on a foil tray on a barbecue for about 8 minutes on each side. **Makes about 8 burgers**

Vegetarian kebabs

To make the sauce, heat the oil and fry the onion and mushrooms for 8 minutes, stirring occasionally. Blend in a food processor for 30 seconds. Add the peanuts and blend for a further 30 seconds until fairly smooth. Return to the pan with the remaining ingredients. Bring to the boil, then simmer for 10 minutes.

Thread the vegetables on to skewers. Brush with the oil and lemon juice. Cook on a barbecue (or under a preheated grill) for about 10 minutes, turning two or three times and brushing with oil and lemon juice. Serve with the peanut sauce. **Serves 8**

Top: Mushroom parcels; Vegetarian Brazil nut burgers (centre); Vegetarian kebabs (front and on plate, with sauce).

INGREDIENTS

8-12 large open mushrooms
50 g (2 oz) butter

FILLING

425 g (15 oz) can chickpeas, drained
1 bunch spring onions, very finely chopped
1 small red pepper, seeded and very finely chopped
few drops of hot pepper sauce

15 ml (1 tbsp) oil
1 leek, very finely chopped
225 g (8 oz) courgettes, very finely chopped
350 g (12 oz) open cup mushrooms, very finely chopped
2.5 ml (½ tsp) chilli powder
125 g (4 oz) Brazil nuts, very finely chopped
50 g (2 oz) wheat flakes, crushed
1 egg (size 4), beaten

8 mini corn-on-the-cob
125 g (4 oz) courgettes, cut into 2.5 cm (1 inch) lengths
450 g (1 lb) chestnut mushrooms
8 button onions
45 ml (3 tbsp) oil
45 ml (3 tbsp) lemon juice

SAUCE

30 ml (2 tbsp) oil
1 small onion, chopped
225 g (8 oz) chestnut mushrooms, chopped
125 g (4 oz) unsalted peanuts
150 ml (¼ pint) water
30 ml (2 tbsp) soy sauce
few drops of hot pepper sauce

Mushroom crown

Stir the mushrooms, thyme and garlic into the bread mix. Stir in enough warm water to form not too soft a dough. Knead well for 5 minutes. Divide into 8 and shape into balls. Arrange on a lightly oiled baking sheet in a ring, leaving a small gap between each ball. Cover with oiled cling film. Leave in a warm place for about 35 minutes. Brush the dough with milk, then sprinkle sesame seeds over the top. Bake in a preheated 220°C (425°F/gas mark 7) oven for about 20 minutes. **Makes 8**

INGREDIENTS

275 g (10 oz) closed cup mushrooms, finely chopped
5 ml (1 tsp) chopped fresh thyme
1 large clove garlic, crushed
275 g (10 oz) white bread mix
about 100 ml (4 fl oz) warm water
milk
sesame seeds

Mushroom cheese spread

Melt the butter and cook the mushrooms for about 5 minutes. Turn into a food processor and blend until fairly smooth. Add the remaining ingredients and blend for a further 30 seconds. Turn into a dish and chill until required. Transport in a chill bag. **Serves 4**

50 g (2 oz) unsalted butter
350 g (12 oz) closed cup mushrooms, chopped
150 g (5 oz) Cheshire cheese, grated
10 ml (2 tsp) horseradish mustard
30 ml (2 tbsp) natural yogurt

Three-minute mushroom salad

Put all the dressing ingredients into a screw-top jar and shake well. Pour the dressing over the mushrooms and stir gently until they are well coated. Store in an airtight container in the refrigerator. Transport in a chill bag. **Serves 4**

450 g (1 lb) button mushrooms
DRESSING
75 ml (5 tbsp) olive oil
30 ml (2 tbsp) red wine vinegar
2.5 ml (½ tsp) dry mustard
5 ml (1 tsp) finely chopped fresh herbs
2.5 ml (½ tsp) sugar
salt and pepper

Top right: Mushroom crown; Pickled mushrooms in oil (in jar; recipe on page 78); Three-minute mushroom salad (centre); Mushroom cheese spread (bottom left).

Pickled Mushrooms
in Oil

Chilled mushroom mousse

Melt the butter and cook the onion and mushrooms for about 3 minutes. Stir in the milk gradually, then leave to cool. Dissolve the gelatine according to the packet instructions; cool, then whisk into the mushroom mixture. Leave in a cool place until just beginning to set, then beat in the remaining ingredients. Turn into a 900 ml (1½ pint) mould. Chill until set. To serve dip the mould into hot water for a few seconds, then invert on to a serving plate. Garnish with sliced mushrooms and chopped aspic jelly. **Serves 6-8**

INGREDIENTS

25 g (1 oz) unsalted butter
1 large onion, very finely chopped
350 g (12 oz) closed cup mushrooms, very finely chopped
300 ml (½ pint) milk
10 ml (2 tsp) powdered gelatine
15 ml (1 tbsp) water
30 ml (2 tbsp) creamed horseradish
150 ml (¼ pint) soured cream

GARNISH

sliced mushrooms
chopped aspic jelly

Glazed mushroom flan

Spread the base of the flan case with the wholegrain mustard. Trim the stalks off the mushrooms close to the caps. Reserve about 12 mushrooms. Chop the remaining mushrooms together with the stalks. Heat the oil and cook the whole mushrooms first. Drain well on absorbent kitchen paper. Cook the remaining chopped mushrooms and drain well.

Scatter the chopped mushrooms over the base of the flan. Beat the cheese, eggs, parsley and seasoning together, then turn into flan case. Bake in a preheated 180°C (350°F/gas mark 4) oven for 30 minutes. Leave to cool, then arrange the cooked whole mushrooms over the flan. Sprinkle the gelatine over the stock, then stir until the gelatine has dissolved. When the glaze is beginning to set, brush over the mushrooms. Chill until set. **Serves 6-8**

1 cooked 25 cm (10 inch) pastry flan case
15 ml (1 tbsp) wholegrain mustard
350 g (12 oz) open cup mushrooms, wiped
60 ml (4 tbsp) oil
350 g (12 oz) cottage cheese
2 eggs (size 4), beaten
15 ml (1 tbsp) chopped fresh parsley
salt and freshly milled black pepper
10 ml (2 tsp) powdered gelatine
200 ml (7 fl oz) very hot clear vegetable stock

Left: Chilled mushroom mousse; Glazed mushroom flan (right).

Microwave Recipes

All the recipes in this chapter have been cooked in a 650 watt microwave with turntable and variable power. Mushrooms cook particularly well in a microwave. It takes just 2 minutes to cook 225 g (8 oz) mushrooms on High. If cooked in a little stock, this quantity accounts for only 68 calories. Mushrooms also taste delicious cooked in a little garlic butter.

Chilled mushrooms

Put the oil, wine, bay leaves, coriander seeds and grated rind from the oranges into a 2 litre (3½ pint) glass bowl. Cook, uncovered, on High for 3 minutes. Add the mushrooms and cover with a glass plate. Cook on Medium for 3 minutes. Remove from the microwave, stir with a wooden spoon, return to the microwave and cook on Medium for a further 3 minutes. Transfer the mushrooms to another bowl, using a slotted spoon. Strain the cooking liquor, season and pour over the mushrooms. Remove the pith from the oranges and cut the flesh into slices. Stir into the mushrooms, cover, cool, then chill for 6 hours. **Serves 8**

INGREDIENTS

30 ml (2 tbsp) vegetable oil
150 ml (¼ pint) white wine
2 bay leaves
8 coriander seeds
2 small (or 1 large) oranges
675 g (1½ lb) button mushrooms
GARNISH
sprig of parsley

Warm mushroom salad

Spin or pat the spinach dry, then shred into a large bowl. Add the onion, red pepper and toast cubes, and mix well. Put the oil and garlic into a large glass dish. Cover and cook on High for 45 seconds. Stir in the lemon juice, seasoning and mushrooms. Cover and cook on High for 3 minutes, stirring halfway through the cooking. Stir the mushrooms into the spinach. Cover and cook on High for 1½ minutes. Toss and serve. **Serves 4-6**

350 g (12 oz) fresh spinach, tough stalks and yellow leaves discarded
1 onion, thinly sliced
1 red pepper, seeded and finely sliced
3 slices granary bread, toasted and cut into cubes
45 ml (3 tbsp) olive oil
2 cloves garlic, crushed
45 ml (3 tbsp) lemon juice
450 g (1 lb) closed cup mushrooms, sliced

Right: Warm mushroom salad.

Baked potatoes

Prick the potatoes all over with a fork, then cook on High for 20 minutes. Meanwhile, pour the oil into a large glass bowl, add the garlic and mushrooms, and stir gently to coat the mushrooms. Stir in the bacon and chives. Cover. Remove the cooked potatoes from the microwave and wrap each one in foil. Set aside. Cook the mushrooms and bacon on High for 5 minutes. Stir, then cook on High for a further 2 minutes. Slit the potato skins and scoop out the centres. Mash the potato and mix with the mushrooms and bacon, together with their juices. Season to taste. Fill the potatoes with the mixture and serve with a green salad. **Serves 4**

INGREDIENTS

4 medium baking potatoes
15 ml (1 tbsp) oil
1 clove garlic, crushed
225 g (8 oz) chestnut mushrooms, sliced
2 rashers bacon, chopped
15 ml (1 tbsp) dried chives

Mushroom scramble

Put the mushrooms in a large glass dish. Add 5 ml (1 tsp) water. Cover and cook on High for 2 minutes. Meanwhile, beat together the eggs, milk and seasoning in a glass jug. Add the butter. Cook on High for 2½-3 minutes, stirring once. Arrange the mushrooms, cap side down, on the toast and spoon the scrambled egg on to the mushrooms. Serve immediately. (The ingredients can be increased to serve more people. However, scrambled eggs are best cooked in small quantities and eaten at once.) **Serves 1**

2 large open cup mushrooms
2 eggs (size 4)
30 ml (2 tbsp) milk
15 g (½ oz) butter, cut into four pieces
1 slice toast

Mushrooms Provençal

Put the oil in a glass bowl with the onion, garlic, herbs and seasoning. Cover with a glass plate and cook on High for 2 minutes. Stir in the tomatoes and mushrooms. Cover and cook on High for 4 minutes, stirring halfway through the cooking. Serve with the tagliatelle. **Serves 4-6**

15 ml (1 tbsp) oil
1 large onion, finely chopped
1 clove garlic, crushed
2.5 ml (½ tsp) mixed fresh thyme and sage, chopped
4 large ripe tomatoes, peeled, halved, seeded and flesh finely chopped
450 g (1 lb) button mushrooms, halved
250 g (9 oz) tagliatelle, cooked and drained

Right: Mushrooms Provençal.

Savoury mushrooms

Put the butter in a small glass dish and cook on Medium for 45 seconds. Remove the tips of the mushroom stalks and chop them finely. Put the mushroom caps in a large glass dish. Make the bread into crumbs and put into a bowl with the mushroom stalks, herbs, half the garlic, ham, cheese and seasoning. Bind together with the egg and about a third of the butter.

Divide the stuffing between the mushroom caps. Add the remaining garlic to the remaining butter and pour over the mushrooms. Cook on High for 5-6 minutes depending on the size of the mushrooms. Serve on toast. **Serves 4**

INGREDIENTS

125 g (4 oz) butter
8 large open mushrooms
3-4 slices brown or white bread
30 ml (2 tbsp) chopped parsley
2.5 ml (½ tsp) fresh rosemary
2 cloves garlic, crushed
125 g (4 oz) ham, finely chopped
50 g (2 oz) Cheddar cheese, grated
1 egg (size 4)
8 rounds of toast

Creamed mushrooms

Melt the butter on High for ½ minute. Add the mushrooms and cook on High for 2 minutes, stirring after 1 minute. Blend together the soured cream, mustard, Worcestershire sauce and tomato purée. Stir the mixture into the mushrooms. Cook on Low for 3 minutes until thoroughly heated, but do not allow to boil. Season to taste, garnish with oregano and serve with wholemeal toast as a starter or snack. **Serves 4**

15 g (½ oz) butter
350 g (12 oz) closed cup mushrooms, thickly sliced
150 ml (¼ pint) soured cream
7.5 ml (1½ tsp) wholegrain mustard
15 ml (1 tbsp) Worcestershire sauce
15 ml (1 tbsp) tomato purée
toast

Light mushroom soup

Cook the butter in a 2 litre (3½ pint) glass bowl on High for 1 minute. Add the onion and mushrooms, and stir well to coat with the butter. Cover and cook on High for 5 minutes. Stir in the milk, stock, potato, nutmeg and seasoning. Cover and cook on High for 10 minutes. Purée in a blender and stir in the cream. Cook on Medium for 1 minute. Serve hot or chilled. **Serves 6**

25 g (1 oz) butter
1 onion, chopped
450 g (1 lb) closed cup mushrooms, chopped
450 ml (¾ pint) skimmed milk
300 ml (½ pint) chicken stock
125 g (4 oz) potato, chopped
2.5 ml (½ tsp) ground nutmeg
150 ml (¼ pint) single cream

Top left: Light mushroom soup; Savoury mushrooms (top right); Creamed mushrooms (bottom).

Trout in creamy mushroom and celery sauce

Put the oil and celery into a glass mixing bowl. Cover with a glass plate. Cook on High for 2 minutes. Stir in the mushrooms, cover and cook on High for a further 3 minutes. Stir in the chopped tarragon and grated lemon rind. Stir in the soured cream and seasoning gradually.

Arrange the trout in a shallow dish, put a sprig of tarragon and slice of lemon inside each trout, then cover with the mushroom mixture. Cover and cook on Medium for 20 minutes, turning after 10 minutes. Stand for 3 minutes before serving with new potatoes and green beans. **Serves 4**

INGREDIENTS

15 ml (1 tbsp) oil
3 sticks celery, finely chopped
225 g (8 oz) closed cup mushrooms, sliced
30 ml (2 tbsp) chopped fresh tarragon
grated rind of 1 large lemon
150 ml (1/4 pint) soured fresh cream
Four 350 g (12 oz) trout, cleaned
4 sprigs fresh tarragon
4 slices lemon

Salmon steaks in mushroom sauce

Put the flour in a glass bowl and mix in the milk gradually, first making a smooth paste, then adding it more quickly and whisking all the time. Add the bay leaf, mace, seasoning and butter. Cook on High for 7-10 minutes until the sauce has boiled and thickened, whisking once halfway through the cooking time. Add the mushrooms and cook on High for a further minute. Cover and keep warm.

Cook the salmon steaks, covered, on High for 8 minutes. Stand for 5 minutes. Reheat the sauce for 1-2 minutes and pour around the fish. Garnish with lemon and parsley. **Serves 4**

40 g (1½ oz) plain flour
600 ml (1 pint) milk
1 bay leaf
blade of mace
25 g (1 oz) butter
225 g (8 oz) button mushrooms
4 salmon steaks
GARNISH
lemon
parsley

Right: Salmon steaks in mushroom sauce.

Coq au vin

Put the oil, garlic and shallots into a large glass bowl. Cover and cook on High for 1 minute. Add the bacon and cook on High for a further minute. Add the mushrooms, stir well and cook on High for 2 minutes. Pour over the wine and chicken stock, and add the bouquet garni. Coat the chicken drumsticks in the flour and arrange in a separate glass dish. Cook the chicken, uncovered, on High for 8 minutes. Pour over the wine and mushroom mixture. Cover and cook on High for 6 minutes, then on Low for 30 minutes, stirring once halfway through the cooking time. If the chicken is not tender, cook, covered, on Low for a further 10 minutes. Stand for 5 minutes before serving garnished with chopped parsley. **Serves 4**

INGREDIENTS

15 ml (1 tbsp) oil
1 clove garlic, finely chopped
8 shallots
4 rashers bacon, chopped
350 g (12 oz) button mushrooms
450 ml (¾ pint) red wine
150 ml (¼ pint) hot chicken stock
bouquet garni
8 chicken drumsticks
30 ml (2 tbsp) plain flour

GARNISH

chopped parsley

Mushroom and cauliflower au gratin

Put the cauliflower florets into a large glass bowl. Add 45 ml (3 tbsp) hot water. Cover and cook on High for 12 minutes. Set aside. Meanwhile, put the mushrooms and butter into a large glass jug and cook on High for 3 minutes. Strain the water from the cauliflower. Add the mushrooms to the cauliflower, reserving the butter and juices in the jug. Add the flour and mustard to the jug and whisk in the milk. Cook on High for 3 minutes, stirring once during the cooking time. Add cheese, stir well, then pour over the cauliflower and mushrooms. Cook, uncovered, on High for 5 minutes. **Serves 4**

1 medium cauliflower, broken into florets
350 g (12 oz) chestnut mushrooms, sliced
50 g (2 oz) butter
25 g (1 oz) plain flour
5 ml (1 tsp) dry mustard
250 ml (8 fl oz) milk
50 g (2 oz) Cheddar cheese, grated

Left: Mushroom and cauliflower au gratin; Coq au vin (right).